SIMPLE MINDS

SIMPLE MINDS

Adam Sweeting

SIDGWICK & JACKSON
LONDON

First published in Great Britain in 1988 by Sidgwick & Jackson Limited

ISBN 0-283-99581-5

Typeset by Hewer Text Composition Services, Edinburgh
Printed by Adlard & Son Ltd, The Garden City Press
for Sidgwick & Jackson Limited
1 Tavistock Chambers, Bloomsbury Way,
London WC1A 2SG

ACKNOWLEDGMENTS

Thanks and without whom . . .

Ian Cranna (painstaking)
Elly Smith (shuttle diplomacy)
Derek Forbes (facts, gossip and snaps)
Brian McGee (different perspective)
David Henderson (lowdown)
Jane Henderson (insight)
Bruce Findlay (lunch)
John Leckie ('sixth member')
Peter Walsh (big dream sound)
Steve Lillywhite (wilder)
Hugh Jones (new slant)
Steve Hillage (vibes and empathy)
Jimmy Iovine (enthusiasm)
Lenny Love, wherever he is
Frank Gallagher (one for my baby)
Melody Maker (1981–1986)
Peter McArthur (pics)
Daniela Soave (short history of Scotland)
Paul Rider, Adele Carmichael (inexhaustible patience)
The Laird of Queensferry (life and times)
The band (when all is said and done)
Amstrad (word processors to the people)

And, of course, Gill for her merciless criticism and microwave
cooking

v

INTRODUCTION

It was the summer of 1986, and everything about Simple Minds was big. Sales of their latest album, *Once Upon A Time*, were booming. They'd filled stadiums and arenas in America and Europe. They'd already sold out Wembley Arena and a batch of dates in Glasgow and Birmingham, and now they'd come back for two shows at Milton Keynes Bowl, a muddy open-air hollow where the looming grey clouds formed a lid for the smell of hamburgers and burning fat.

The Wembley shows earlier in the year had revealed a deafeningly loud Simple Minds who trampled older material like 'Promised You A Miracle' or 'Love Song' mercilessly with their new megaton sound. New songs, 'Once Upon A Time' or 'Alive And Kicking', had been built with the new global dynamics in mind and stood up to the treatment better, while guest vocalist Robin Clark proved a much better belter of a song than Jim Kerr. But anybody who'd turned up hoping for a glimpse of the mysterious Minds of *Empires And Dance* or *Sons And Fascination* must have thought they'd fallen into a time-warp, or had something put into their beer.

The Minds at Milton Keynes had all the trappings of impersonal multinational rock, dimensions removed from the Glasgow pubs where it had all begun. The stage was a towering web of lighting gantries, scaffolding and PA equipment, flanked by the giant dove-in-the-hand motif which represented Simple Minds' commitment to Amnesty International; an admirable cause, of course, but the dove was looking more like a tattered old pigeon after being lugged halfway round the world.

Out in the crowd, the ground was covered with the usual festival debris – split and crushed plastic beer glasses, bumper-sized empty Coke bottles, half-chewed burgers wrapped in papier-mâché bread. A newspaper called the *Chronicle & Echo* previewed the Minds and supporting acts in muddy pictures and turgid prose, and got the picture captions of the group members wrong. "Gradually," it said, "through eight albums and innumerable tours, Simple Minds have picked up thousands of relieved music lovers fed up with the mindless pop pap dominating the music scene these days." Like the event itself, the sentiment felt detached and secondhand.

Bogus "official" vendors sold a patched-together tour brochure consisting of out-of-date photographs and old music press interviews, sources uncredited. It was a complete racket, but a very difficult one to combat. Backstage, in their portable cabins behind a twee white picket fence, the band were oblivious to it. One open-air festival looks much like another, after all.

As a prelude to the Minds' homecoming British dates back in February, the TV show *The Tube* had presented Simple Minds live from Rotterdam. It was the first time British audiences had had a chance to see them in many months, and when the opening song, 'Waterfront', plodded on and on without getting within sniffing distance of a climax, it was evident that a great many things had changed. Simple Minds had become what their critics had long claimed they were anyway – pomp-rockers, repackaged and trimmed in American chrome.

Kerr never bothered to deny it. The band had been called the New Genesis so often that they'd started referring to themselves as "the new Barclay James Harvest" for a bit of variety. He liked telling the story about how he and guitarist Charlie Burchill went to see Genesis in Glasgow when Peter Gabriel was still singing with them, and how you could get in free by making sure your ticket didn't get punched, then putting it in an envelope and throwing it out through the lavatory window for someone else to pick up and re-use. We *liked* pomp-rock, he explained. If you don't like us that's your problem.

Simple Minds' manager, Bruce Findlay, isn't averse to a little dinosaur imagery, either. He always knew his boys would be monsters one day. "They have always been, in my opinion, Genesis, Pink Floyd and The Beatles rolled into one, artistically and commercially," he raved, as long ago as 1983. "They had that kind of potential. I could see them becoming huge."

In essence, Kerr's attitude now is that he's changed, Simple Minds have grown, and if you don't like it, it's tough. If it's a choice between losing thousands of old fans and gaining millions of new ones, he'll stick with the new ones, even if that means resorting to the most obvious stadium-pleasing tactics. To reach crowds on this scale, spectacle takes pride of place over musical considerations.

"You know, twenty people standing spectating is one thing," Kerr said later, when the tour was over. "Fifty thousand standing spectating is something else. I think it's good to give them a chance to come into it. I do realize it's very, very obvious, but I'm not trying to break any new kind of performance barriers here. That's what Laurie Anderson's for. Sometimes live, on a good night, those things will work. On a bad night, they'll seem unnecessary and overblown and over the top and stuff."

And, he pointed out, this was just the latest phase in the band's development. They'd never stood still for long in the past, so why should this period be any different?

"If people did like the band and don't now for whatever reason, initially – *initially* – you feel kind of sad. The second thing is that I think, well, a lot of the people criticizing us were people who'd never really spent the time checking us out. And the third thing is that, well, maybe we'll come back and play in clubs. Who knows?

"This is a period we're going through just now, and I think with any artist who does a substantial body of work there's gonna be all these phases in it that involve good and bad, where you get it wrong or get it right, where you blow it, where you do something amazing and then fall on your arse with the next thing. In terms of the press and even of the fans, there's been so many phases with Simple Minds. In the initial phase, with our first two albums, nobody liked us. Then we started winning polls here and there.

"It's the mundaneness of the complaints that gets to me. It's

3

just so fucking obvious. I think a lot of people just don't like big business, and the last phase of Simple Minds was a big machine. But I think just now, for the first time, what you got onstage was the same as you got offstage. There was no act or mystery. As I've said before, it doesn't matter if you're The Fall or Frank Sinatra – if you say you're gonna be onstage in Belgium on Tuesday at nine o'clock, it's showbusiness. I agree it's up to you what stage you take it to, but it's undoubtedly showbusiness, and I realize that.''

Through a combination of hard work, some excellent records and a handy slice of luck, by 1986 Simple Minds had arrived as one of the world's major mainstream rock groups after nearly ten years of touring and recording. At last, American audiences were responding to their videos on MTV and acknowledging that their records sounded great on FM radio. Simple Minds have made a sequence of LPs that still stand up as some of the most distinctive of their time, and even they will acknowledge that they'll be very lucky if they ever make another record as singular and atmospheric as 1982's *New Gold Dream*.

While the group were scarcely unsuccessful even in the early eighties, they were becoming aware that it would be easy for them to fall into the trap of repetition or self-parody that threatened groups who'd once been regarded as their peers and contemporaries, like Echo and the Bunnymen or New Order. In Kerr's view, these were groups who had defined a sound, a look and an attitude, and had then been content to sit back and wait and see what happened.

''We knew we could write these atmospheric backdrops with pulsating basslines, with stream-of-consciousness lyrics over the top,'' he said. ''We realized we could write them till the cows came home, but there was no challenge.'' Their best music was more than that, and more than the sum of its parts, but it couldn't be bettered. The options were simple – change or fade away.

As it began to appear that the Bunnymen were treading water, New Order were happy to be the big fish in the independent-label pool and Siouxsie and the Banshees were reduced to recording cover versions of elderly rock classics, Simple Minds

4

pushed on towards the most glittering prize of all: America. Once they'd chosen their objective, their transformation into the Simple Minds of today was a matter of hard, simple logic. The same form of natural selection that determines whether you sink or swim, climb or fall, eventually moulds you into the most effective shape for continued survival.

In the same week that Simple Minds were announcing their 1986 British arena dates to the music press, Echo and the Bunnymen started a UK tour of middle-sized venues. The Bunnymen themselves had become aware of their predicament. Being perverse and eccentric is its own reward; it brings few financial ones. It wasn't that many years ago that the Bunnymen looked like being as big, or bigger, than either Simple Minds or U2.

"I think you get to a point where you've got to make some money," said their guitarist, Will Sergeant. "Look at bands like The Fall. They've just whittled away at the same old shit, you know? I really liked The Fall, I thought they were great, but they've just . . . stopped.

"There's a point where you can get so big you can do whatever you want. Like Prince and *Around The World In A Day*. He's probably always wanted to make a weirdo *Sergeant Pepper*-type LP, and he's done it now. He could have done it for his first LP but it would just have been nothing and he wouldn't have been able to do it as well, probably. You can stick to your principles too much and you end up where everyone hates you and thinks you're a dickhead."

Back in 1983, during a bout of songwriting at a snow-bound rehearsal studio in Lincolnshire, Jim Kerr had dropped what, in retrospect, turned out to be a clue to the group's future direction.

"I still think if it's the right band and a hall with 3,000 people crammed together it's great, don't you? When that became crap was when you had a crap band, it was never the lights or the dry ice. The band's either good or they're rubbish, and you shouldn't confuse that."

Four years and four million copies of *Once Upon A Time* later, and with a new live double album just leaping into the charts,

5

Kerr was still expressing himself in strikingly similar terms. "At the end of the day we are a hell of a noise, and it's gonna get out of hand sometimes, and then it's gonna be really good. It's very simple really. You get obsessed with all the technicalities, and whether this stands for this or whether the record company hyped that, but there's only two types of music, and that's good and bad."

CHAPTER 1

When Jim Kerr bought his father a Porsche Carrera with some of the proceeds from *Once Upon A Time*, he probably remembered a rather more humble form of transport which had carried the fledgling Simple Minds to gigs around Glasgow and Edinburgh a decade earlier. It was an old minibus, and at the time it was a real struggle for the group to afford it.

"We bought this bus for about £250," Kerr remembered. "No, it was £350. We got our parents to chip in about fifty quid each. We used to put in three quid each a week – it was a really big thing if you were on the dole, getting £15.50. This bus used to belong to a school for the mentally handicapped, and we did it all up."

The band was always a team effort, built around a group of schoolfriends from Glasgow and rooted in a closely-knit working class Catholic community. Against the chaotic backdrop of Glasgow's own version of punk rock events taking place around London, family and friends were closely involved and supportive. Once everybody had absorbed the shock of their children wanting to dress up, wear make-up and chance their arm in a notoriously unreliable business, they were filled with pride and a determination to help.

It was the familiar story of music representing a rare possibility of escape from surroundings which offered little prospect of self-betterment, let alone a high-flying professional career. Getting out of Glasgow wasn't easy, as Jim's grandfather had discovered. He'd sold up and sailed to New York in the twenties, and had made himself a fortune during the free-for-all Prohibition

7

years. But then he'd lost it all again during the Wall Street Crash, and returned, embittered and poor, to Glasgow.

Times hadn't changed that much. Kerr remembered how his father, a bricklayer, had been greeted with derision by his workmates when he'd been caught reading a book, or mentioned that he'd been to the theatre. Jim was named after his father (who's usually known as Jimmy), and though neither of them received an academic education, both share an instinctive intellectual curiosity.

Jimmy, a lapsed Catholic, had communist sympathies which his wife Irene preferred him to keep quiet about. Jimmy later joined Amnesty International, a move which would rub off on Jim and was partly responsible for Simple Minds' support for the movement on their 1985–6 world tour. But Jim didn't want to be cramped, intellectually or geographically, in the same way as his father had been. Had it not been for the band, his future would have been either manual work or the dole. Bruce Springsteen probably felt much the same about his hometown of Freehold, New Jersey.

But the band couldn't cut away their roots if they tried, and today, Jim Kerr regards the word "expatriate" as the worst insult you can throw at him. The New Musical Express were forced to print an apology when they alleged that after his marriage to Chrissie Hynde of the Pretenders in 1984, he'd bought a new home in Los Angeles.

"I never knew anything about working class or middle class or rich because everybody was just the same," he says now. "It was like a total class, and so you didn't think about various degrees. Up to a point – and I'm really telling the truth here – I've always felt very, very rich, I think, because I never felt troubled.

"I'm very lucky that I've never had to face tragedy in any sense. I've been brought up with an amazing family that totally comprehended each other, a lot of warmth, a lot of love, and then I went straight from that into this band which was formed from mates and friendship. I'm very kind of sheltered, so I've always been rich."

The nucleus of the original Simple Minds was Kerr, guitarist Charlie Burchill and drummer Brian McGee. All three attended

Holyrood school, where they first got together in 1973, though Burchill and Kerr went back even further, having been near neighbours in the city's Toryglen district. The Kerr family had once lived in the Gorbals, the notoriously tough Glasgow slum where the buildings dated back to the Victorian era. Jim had been born there on 9 July 1959, and remembers the area with something like nostalgia.

"There were some knives and razors, but never guns. The important thing was not to get involved. A common sight would be a man and a woman fighting in the street, drunk, and the guy would be giving her a real seeing to, but when anybody intervened they'd both turn round and tell him to mind his own fucking business. It was all about going out to have a drink and a fight and then becoming mates again."

Underlying the drinking and violence, there was a unique sense of community and mutual support. People were poor, but did their best to make sure that whatever there was in the way of luxuries was shared around equally. "If you worked in a TV warehouse, then you stole colour TVs for everyone," Jim remembered. "And there were all these incredible characters. If you wanted a pedigree dog, you'd go to Brown the dog stealer. It was all he did, steal dogs. You'd tell him what breed and colour you wanted and he'd scout around the richer neighbourhoods until he found one." In the late sixties, the Kerrs were moved to the new high-rise development in Toryglen, while the local council finally bulldozed their old estate. Of course, the legends of the district live on.

Kerr remembered how he first met Burchill. "There was a building site at the bottom of the street and Charlie was playing in the sand-mound, making pies and stuff like that. I was eight and he was seven. Charlie says his first memory of me at Holyrood school was when I was having a fight with a guy called Tommy Lanagan, and I was wasting him. I remember being frightened to fight him because he had dockman's shoes."

Kerr also recalls, rather unkindly, his first sight of Brian McGee. "I remember McGee coming into the class at secondary school and laughing at him cos he wore glasses. I remember him

9

being sent off at football and he started crying – he had a total tantrum.''

The adolescent Kerr became infatuated with David Bowie and went through his own glam phase, where he wore ''big boots, mascara and painted nails'' and worried about getting beaten up by the hard-drinking men on the building sites where he'd work to save up some money in the school holidays. Kerr was painfully shy, but paradoxically had a broad exhibitionist streak too.

Jim and Charlie made their first-ever public appearance in their first-ever band in front of a group of five-year-old orphans. Charlie says, ''Me and Jim were in bands that were really just like me and him and sort of friends, and we had all these different names – we changed names every three days. Then we split away from all these people and went hitch-hiking. We went to Europe and hitched right through Europe to Italy, then came back up the other way through Holland. No, in fact we got split up – I came back via Holland and Jim came back via Belgium. We'd just left school.''

The first regular group the trio were in was Johnny and the Self Abusers, an unwieldy semi-punk seven-piece who scratched together as many gigs as they could at places like the Doune Castle pub and Zhivago's Disco. The Abusers had two vocalists, Kerr and John Milarky, and played cover versions of songs like The Ramones' 'Blitzkrieg Bop', Chris Spedding's 'Pogo Dancing', and 'Waiting' by the Doctors of Madness. Obviously it couldn't last, but Glasgow had never seen anything quite like it.

Burchill has bizarre memories of John Milarky, whose behaviour proved something of an inspiration to all of them. ''We went round to his house and it was a pure fuckin' riot. He said, 'I've got this song called 'Pablo Picasso' [not the John Cale one], and he just stood there and he started playing it. He had a brush coming through from his living room with a microphone on the end of it. And he just stood there like that, singing through a guitar amplifier. The words were, like, 'Pablo Picasso, all the girls think you're an asshole'. It was brilliant. We just sat there and went, 'that's fuckin' incredible!'

''But there was like this real division in the Self Abusers, cos me, Brian and Jim were working class and came from a housing scheme and the others were from privately-owned houses and wealthy parents. But the attitudes were all really crazy and right into it. We started off doing cover versions of Sex Pistols songs and old Kinks songs and 'Baby's On Fire' by Eno, and a lot of Velvet Underground tracks. Then we gradually started writing our own stuff."

It soon became apparent that Kerr and Burchill were the ones with the greater songwriting potential. Kerr was already getting used to the role of the arty, introverted one, sitting up all night in the kitchen of his parents' council flat, writing words by the light of a small lamp. The flat was cramped and had glass doors, and Jim didn't want to wake up the rest of the family.

Burchill, meanwhile, was restless, bursting with a kinetic energy which could be quite exhausting for the people he came in contact with. He was to become the eccentric of the band, the one who was sometimes spotted wearing wrappers from Hovis loaves on his feet, always raring to go to the next gig, the next party, the next interview. He could spend half an hour telling you something one day with incontrovertible zeal, then the next day he'd tell you exactly the opposite with equal enthusiasm.

Charlie first started playing guitar when he was fifteen, at the same time as his elder brother Jamie. His first instrument carried the brand name Nymph, and had been bought with 3,500 cigarette coupons which his mother had saved up through an arduous schedule of smoking. Even today, he still appears to have little need for sleep, and never leaves home without a guitar and a small portable amplifier.

"I can remember the very earliest days of learning about the harmony between the guitar and the bass," he said. "I can remember the satisfaction even from the early days. We never knew any songs and we'd just play anything, we couldn't play guitars. There was a John Mayall album we'd listen to, *John Mayall's Bluesbreakers* – I hate John Mayall and I hated that record but the start of it was classic, with the bass playing this sort of progression. It was the only thing I'd heard at the time which had different parts for different instruments. We played that and learned it, and we heard the harmony between the bass and

11

the guitar and we were going, 'Yes! It works!' It was the fascination of when something becomes a reality."

Jim Kerr has never learned to play an instrument, despite efforts to find his way around a keyboard, but has always fulfilled an indefinable but important motivating role. "Somebody can say to me, 'you're a shit guitar player,' or something like that," Charlie said, "or, 'I don't like your guitar playing at all,' but that would sort of bounce off me because of my brother's reaction and Jim's reaction in the early days. They were like two big powerhouses behind me, and I would just say to myself, 'I think I've got an imagination that I hope these people who are criticizing me would never be able to realize,' because if they *did* realize then I'd begin to get worried that I was dropping to a certain level."

Neither Jim nor Charlie ever seriously considered getting a "proper job", though Kerr briefly tried his hand at joinery while Burchill trained to be a plumber for six months, and was a motor mechanic for one afternoon. They weren't interested in following in their parents' footsteps. Jim's father was a bricklayer, Charlie's worked for British Rail. Jim's mother worked in a cake shop, Charlie's in a betting shop. Their backgrounds weren't wealthy but they were solid and, despite a traditional allegiance to the Labour Party, extremely conservative. Although their neighbours and relatives were liable to regard any form of artistic endeavour as pretentious or plain idiotic, as far as they were concerned the future was with the group, and the pair began to dominate the songwriting within the Self Abusers.

"'Pablo Picasso' was the only good song John Milarky had," said Burchill, "and eventually we got rid of all his songs and added the rest of the songs ourselves. But it was a great period, it helped shape a lot of the attitudes we've got now. You just couldn't get banal about anything, cos it started off on such a high and wild note."

As Brian McGee recalled, "If it wasn't for the punk thing happening, Simple Minds would never be where they are today, because we wouldn't have had the guts to go out and do a gig. Before punk happened, we said, 'we'll do this, we'll do that,' but we couldn't pluck up enough courage to go onstage and do it

12

anywhere. Punk was a free invitation to anybody, and we just did it from then on."

McGee (whose younger brother Owen would hit the charts in later years under the pseudonym Owen Paul) seemed to need little encouragement to do the craziest things, as many later exploits would demonstrate. It was he who threw a wellington boot through the front window of the Milarky household one night in a fit of rage, though his crime was uncovered the following day when he picked up Milarky in his father's van for a rehearsal. In the back were three pairs of wellington boots plus an odd one.

Somehow, the Self Abusers came to the notice of London-based Chiswick Records, with whom they recorded their November 1977 single 'Saints And Sinners'/'Dead Vandals'. With impeccable timing, the group split up on the day the record was released.

While the Milarky faction went off to form Cuban Heels, Kerr, Burchill and McGee assembled Simple Minds, Mark 1. The group played their first-ever gig at Glasgow's Satellite City on 17 January 1978, where they supported Birmingham reggae band Steel Pulse. Alongside the basic trio, they'd recruited Mick MacNeil on keyboards, Duncan Barnwell on second guitar and another ex-Self Abuser, Tony Donald, on bass. Tony's uncle owned a lampshade factory where the group had held their early rehearsals.

MacNeil had been recruited after a tip-off from an ex-girlfriend of Burchill's. Mick's family originally came from the island of Barra, in the Hebrides, where Gaelic is still spoken (you can see some old friends of the MacNeils in the Ealing comedy *Whisky Galore*, which was filmed on nearby South Uist). "It's a brilliant place," said Mick. "Great for getting your head together. I had a cousin who nearly ended up a nutcase, but he went up there and in six months he was brand new again."

Mick was the quiet one of the group, possibly suspicious of language when music was a much more reliable bet. The story is that he had trouble speaking English when he first went to school in Glasgow. "Well, I could a wee bit, but it was really bad," he allows. "Now I can't speak English or Gaelic."

13

"Mick had a Protestant upbringing and his was the weirdest of the lot," Kerr said mischievously, some years later. "His old man used to get drunk and talk to the dead. You'd go round there and his mum would be watching the telly, and his old man would be lying on the table talking to the dead, and Mick would be sitting there in the corner with his synthesizer going, 'Och, will ye shut up.'"

For all that, music ran in the MacNeil family. Mick attended a music school from the age of ten, where he learned to play the accordion and also gained a sturdy education in musical theory.

"There'd be maybe ten accordionists, and it would be all kinds of classical stuff like the Skater's Waltz or something, with each person playing a different part. You'd get given a piece of music and you'd have a week to learn so much of it, then you'd go through it with the teacher at weekends. I used to get into it for maybe a page and then I'd get bored, and start improvizing it without actually bothering with the music. The teacher would say 'you've got a good ear but you need to stick to the way it's written'. He never used to encourage us to improvize."

MacNeil's willingness to experiment probably stemmed from the various musical noises which filled the MacNeil household at one time or another. "There's seven in the family and everybody's played something or other at some time," he said. "My mum and dad really encouraged everybody from when they were dead young to get into it, be it singing in a choir or playing an acoustic guitar. I remember my dad was once asked to sing at this Gaelic choir concert and get a pound for doing it. He'd never done it before and he was dead shy, and he went away and got drunk and never turned up. He was too nervous."

Once, Mick even had a go on the bagpipes. "I gave them to my dad in the end – I couldn't even fill the bag up. You need compressed air, or maybe a bicycle pump. That would be cheating, though, because you need to express it with wind."

MacNeil's quasi-classical training would prove to be an important and ever-expanding influence within the Simple Minds' sound, moving them steadily away from any conventional rock format into richer, more ambiguous textures. He was

14

always convinced that tones could speak just as loudly as words. "With a bit of music with no words on it, it's more difficult to make up your mind about it, about what kind of mood's coming from it," he reflected.

Mick apparently had no idea who people like David Bowie, Lou Reed and Magazine were when he first met up with the Minds, since he didn't listen to the radio or watch *Top Of The Pops* or, indeed, have very much interest in pop music at all. "Up to that point I hadn't been into music outside of Highland music and all that, so it was just like going in and writing brand new," he said. "It was funny, cos everybody would say the keyboards were just like stuff from Magazine and Ultravox and all that, and I'd never really heard their records or anything."

He did some catching up over the years, though you're still more likely to find Ravel or Mozart on his Walkman than Bryan Adams or Run DMC. But he did have a grounding in making music for a living, since he and his brother Danny had played in groups together. As the Barnets, they appeared on the tacky TV show *Junior Showtime* wearing kilts, a memory still guaranteed to make MacNeil blush. In his mid-teens, Mick and his brother found a couple of other musicians and played at local social clubs, weddings and assorted functions. He didn't enjoy the kind of music they had to play, but at least it earned him enough money to buy his first synthesizer. It was a primitive Korg instrument, and Mick bought it when he was sixteen.

Kerr says, "We were going 'there's this guy in Glasgow with a synthesizer! A real fuckin' synth! We'll have to get him to join no matter how good he is!' As it happened he was brilliant anyway.

"We were playing in the Mars Bar in Glasgow but we weren't making any money. We told Mick we'd give him three days to think it over, and in that three days we got our first-ever chance to do a big gig, supporting the Stranglers. It was our first taste of playing a big hall, and we said to Mick 'you've *got* to stay'."

MacNeil took a little persuading that joining the band was his best bet, since he was also showing promise as an engineering apprentice. His family and friends took the traditional view that some sort of job qualification was only common sense in a time of rising unemployment, and everybody knew that life in a pop group stood every chance of ending in disaster. Mick saw their point, but he also realized that Simple Minds offered creative opportunities he was unlikely to find again.

"It was really good, cos they'd just play and you had to play what was in your head, y'know, and I'd never done that before. I don't think I could have as much freedom somewhere else as I've got here. I was really sick of going round social clubs doing old Drifters songs and that."

So the band had found a keyboard player. Then Tony Donald quit, and Simple Minds went looking for a bass player too. They happened across Derek Forbes, bassist with a group called the Subs, and coincidentally a friend of Barnwell's. It hadn't been long since Forbes had returned from a stint playing both bass and guitar in clubs and discos in the Spanish resort of Lloret de Mar. Barnwell had arrived there from Scotland one day and enthused at length to Forbes about this amazing group called Johnny and the Self Abusers, who at the time were raising hell in a pub called the Doune Castle.

Forbes can (and will) make a long list of his musically-inclined relatives. He had an aunt and uncle who played guitar and banjo at the Glasgow Pavilion at the time of the British folk boom pioneered by Billy Connolly and Hamish Imlach. "And then my cousins all played guitar, and that's what really got me into it." He came close to joining the Navy, but was eventually dissuaded by the recruiting officer. "The guy said, 'Have you any hobbies?' and I said, 'Well, I'm starting to play the guitar.' I was fifteen or sixteen at the time. And he said, 'Well, you'll not have much time for that; if you're not interested don't join.' The guy actually talked me out of joining the Navy, and you'd think they wanted recruits."

Thus spared, Forbes began playing lead guitar with wittily-titled outfits like Moby Dick and Big Dick And The Four Skins. In Lloret de Mar, he did a spot of painting and decorating, and played in a group at night. "All the songs were rubbish, and that was the first time I played bass," he admitted. "It was embarrassing, we used to start off with 'Uno Paloma Blanca' – I used to sing 'I'm a compulsive wanker.' I used to start off

16

playing bass for a couple of hours because the bass player couldn't play bass and sing at the same time, so he went on the guitar and sang. Then I'd go on to lead guitar and start playing it with my teeth and behind my head and all that sort of stuff.''

He might have pottered on happily as a jobbing musician, soaking up the sea and sand in holiday resorts, but from Barnwell's excitable manner he sensed that something was going on back home and returned promptly from Spain. He swiftly joined the Subs, with whom his career was short-lived despite a dramatic week the band spent trapped in a snowbound cottage on their way back from a gig in Stornoway, on the Isle of Lewis. Like the Self Abusers, they too split up shortly after releasing a single, which in their case was 'Gimme Your Heart'/'Party Clothes' on Stiff Records (Stiff OFF-1). ''Scotland's own Subs produced the best of the OFFs (but not the most successful),'' wrote Bert Muirhead, analyzing the label's output in his book *Stiff – the Story of a Record Label* (Blandford).

Forbes had been thinking about becoming a lead guitarist again, but was happy to accept the Minds' offer of playing bass on some demo recordings they planned to make. ''I said I was going to be a guitarist again but I'll play with you as long as you need me. And then my guitar got stolen the day of recording 'Chelsea Girl', and I said, 'well if it's all right with you I'd like to join.' They said great.''

Forbes was already more rock-star minded than the others, an extrovert figure entirely without self-consciousness. If he hadn't become a musician he rather liked the idea of being a professional footballer, though, being a Protestant like MacNeil, he supported Glasgow Rangers while Kerr, Burchill and McGee backed Celtic.

''You shouldn't take it too seriously,'' Forbes observed. ''But it's not for me to say, politics or religion or whatever, me being a mere bass player. I think I've always been the black sheep in my family, because I've always had this burning ambition to make something of myself and make my family proud. When I was about nine I remember I wrote this note, I didn't want anybody to see it, and it said 'I'm going to make my family proud of me

17

one day. If it's not football, I'm just going to make something of myself'. I remember getting embarrassed when my father and brother found it."

"Derek was in the Subs," said Burchill, "and me and Jim had seen him, and we said, 'he's a big fucking show-off and he plays bass like it was a lead guitar, but he's good.' Then we got rid of Duncan, the other guitar player, and that was us. Duncan was a wild guy actually, he had a good attitude. But then, he looked terrible and he started really getting a bit daft. There was no need for two guitars anyway."

But in May, before Barnwell's departure, the Minds recorded a six-song demo tape in Glasgow's budget-priced Ça Va studios, which at that time was equipped with an eight-track tape machine. The songs they cut were 'Act Of Love', 'European Son', 'Cocteau Twins', 'Chelsea Girl', 'Doo Be Doo' and 'Pleasantly Disturbed', all for a total cost of £226. 'European Son' was subsequently replaced by a Self Abusers song, 'Wasteland', when the group went hawking the tape round the London record companies.

Then they went looking for some management, or at least some sort of professional assistance. By now they had a settled line-up, a batch of original material, and a steadily-growing track record of gigs around Glasgow. Locally, they were beginning to build up a reputation, despite their obvious indebtedness to a list of musical idols that included Bowie, Genesis, Roxy Music, Lou Reed and the Velvet Underground, and the Doctors Of Madness. These influences could be detected on the demo tape, but the group had already developed enough poise and presence of their own to impress people who heard the primitive recordings.

CHAPTER 2

Ian Cranna, then based in Edinburgh and writing freelance pieces for the *New Musical Express*, was among the first people to spot the Minds' potential. Originally he'd been contacted by David Henderson, who with his sister Jane looked after Simple Minds' sound, lighting and all-round technical requirements.

"The upshot of this phone call was that a very nervous young man arrived on my doorstep in Edinburgh bearing a tape," Cranna recalled. "It turned out to be Jim Kerr, who left me this cassette which wasn't even in a plastic case. It was in an envelope with the track titles written on the outside. I didn't normally play tapes in the presence of the people who brought them, because it was usually a fairly horrible experience. So eventually, after two days or something, I put this one on, and it was wonderful. It was so completely different from everything else that was going on, not one of those things where you play the first few bars and then immediately reach for the stop button. It still remains one of my most treasured possessions, I think."

Cranna had seen the Self Abusers when they played in a punk package in Edinburgh, and had once been dragged out to a disco in Hamilton to witness a performance by Forbes' band the Subs. "The Abusers did have a real style and pace, sort of like a musical flying junkyard," he reckoned, but maintained a tactful silence about the Subs.

Galvanized by the Minds' demo tape, Cranna made tracks for Glasgow and the Mars Bar where the group had by now

19

secured themselves a residency. He was impressed, to put it mildly.

"The first few early dates of Simple Minds I saw, they were the perfect cross of old and new waves – they had energy, they had melody, they had real sort of depth and commitment which a lot of the other punk acts didn't have. Even then it was quite obvious that Jim Kerr was an outstanding front man. He had real presence, and I thought they were wonderful."

The Mars Bar shows were vivid and spectacular, out of all proportion either to the size of the venue or the achievements of the band up until that time. Kerr: "It was the first time ever that a Glasgow band played a set of their own songs, cos Glasgow bands always played cover versions, right? We would play and the place would be fucking packed – hundreds of people outside, like more than would go and see the Banshees. And we would do the whole thing, dress up and stuff."

The audio-visual experience was augmented by David Henderson's sound mixing and his sister Jane's lights. David had first come across the band in the Johnny and the Self Abusers days, when he'd been working in a Glasgow record shop managed by Scott MacArthur. MacArthur had fulfilled a vaguely managerial role with the Self Abusers for a time, helping to organize their single for the Chiswick label, and had brought David along to a couple of their gigs. When the group split up, MacArthur went off with the Cuban Heels fragment. Meanwhile, David's sister Jane was working as a graphic designer and had made posters of Simple Minds for their Mars Bar dates. When David decided he couldn't handle both sound and lights, he asked Jane if she wanted to have a go at the latter.

Anything went. David would make up his own tapes to play before the band went on, patching together sounds of clocks, musical boxes and bits of Eno records. Jane assembled a revolving perspex head with a flashing blue light from a police car inside it, which would spin in the darkness as the band took the stage, their backs to the audience.

On a good night, the effect could be devastating, and word soon spread throughout Glasgow and beyond about this unique new band. Ian Cranna: "I can remember two punters in particular, completely out of it, on the floor propped up against each other. They'd taped the Minds' set on a portable tape recorder. The sound was dreadful but there they were lying with expressions of bliss on their faces, with the tape recorder perched between them."

Local musicians would come down to see them play too, like the Skids' vocalist, Richard Jobson. Jane Henderson remembers first meeting Jobson when Johnny and the Self Abusers played at a disco in Dunfermline. Brian McGee and guitarist Alan McNeil were trying to steal some PA speakers and asked a passer-by to give them a hand. The passer-by was Jobson, and the PA belonged to the Skids. Despite this, Jobbo became a firm fan and friend of Simple Minds.

The group were entirely ignorant about the processes of the music business. Still, though they would chip in £5 each for Jim or David Henderson to travel to London to take the demo tape round the record companies, they were already determined they wouldn't be tempted to move south in pursuit of lucrative contracts and press attention. They felt instinctively that they had to hone and hammer their music until it was too strong and too personal to be wrenched out of their control by business-men. At that time, they lacked all kinds of basic skills which can ease a young act's passage through the entrails of the music business and the media.

Ian Cranna began to act in an informal advisory capacity, offering a little industry know-how to the ambitious but ill-informed band. "They had no interview technique back then, and it was a long time before they developed one," he said. "I used to put a tape on and leave it, in the hope that after an hour and a half or whatever there'd be an article's worth of material in there. But Jim and Charlie were the two main talkers. My overriding memory of them was their determination. They were going to sit there and create something which was too good to be ignored, that was their phrase – 'something too good to be ignored'."

But since the courteous, precisely-spoken Cranna was simul-taneously studying for a PhD in seventeenth-century Scottish

21

and Dutch relations at Edinburgh University, he wasn't able to travel with the group or attend as many of their performances as he would have liked. Inevitably, they began to be noticed further afield, and before very long they turned up in the office of Bruce Findlay. He ran a record label called Zoom, which was affiliated to Arista, and with his elder brother Brian, owned the Edinburgh-based chain of record shops, Bruce's Records. By this time Findlay had about eight shops and several years of experience in various aspects of the music business.

"They were the best record shops Britain's ever had, and I say it with complete modesty," Bruce reminisced. He's a stocky, bespectacled figure who rarely stops talking and is almost always cheerful. "Shy" is a word whose meaning has never been explained to him. "I did mail order, American imports and bootlegs while Richard Branson was still having his nappies changed. I could have settled down and grown into my middle-age as a successful record shop owner. But I'd have become very frustrated because music became boring – it wasn't boring in 1976, but it was boring in 1972."

Findlay was enough of a local celebrity for the Lord Provost of Edinburgh to ask him to sponsor pop music at the Edinburgh Festival ("which was unheard of"), and he did so in 1973. He assembled a weird collection of acts, from the Incredible String Band and John Martyn to the Chieftains, Gong, and Can, and ended up losing money. He didn't care. "That got me a taste for getting involved with artists. I'd always liked artists anyway, hanging about with groups – I was like a groupie. I was never a frustrated artist or anything, but I did enjoy their company and I did love music and I love the way it's created, and I love the language that people in bands talk."

Through his retailing experience, Findlay had built up contacts with all the record companies, and had an especially good rapport with Island. "In my opinion, Island was the single best independent label Britain had ever produced, and I say this with no apology to Virgin Records. Island were the innovators of it all, because they had that mixture of aggressive capitalism, business common sense, but with beautiful marketing ideas and very tasteful A&R signings. They revolutionized the British record market, and if it hadn't been for Island there wouldn't have been a Virgin.''

Findlay had once had discussions with Island about setting up his own licensed label. Island had been looking for singles-orientated acts while Findlay had high hopes for a group called Cafe Jacques, who he also managed. Cafe Jacques were not a singles band, and no Island deal resulted. Bruce recalled how he'd once driven down to London from Edinburgh to try to negotiate a deal for them with CBS, after the band had just played a gig and were exhausted. It was a salutary experience to be recalled in future years.

"We slotted a couple of keep-awake things back and drove to London, playing 'Set The Controls For The Heart Of The Sun'. We got to London first thing in the morning, the appointment with CBS was at nine thirty, but they didn't make it and we were kept hanging around until one o'clock. When we finally had the meeting I was shattered. I had this neon sign flashing across my forehead – MUG MUG MUG. I was a complete mug and I got taken to the cleaners. I didn't know how to negotiate a deal – I couldn't have organized a piss-up in a brewery at the time. I wore my heart right on my sleeve. I still do, except I'm not a mug any longer.''

For a combination of reasons, Cafe Jacques never fulfilled their promise and split up, while Findlay eventually got his Zoom label organized through Arista. He released records by almost-forgotten names like the Zones, Nightshift and the Questions (the latter would later turn up on Paul Weller's Respond label). Clearly he had the right kind of credentials for a potential manager of Simple Minds, even if his early experiences in management had been marred by naivety.

Kerr and David Henderson came to Edinburgh to see the effervescent Bruce. "The pair of them were wearing eye make-up and very strange hairstyles,'' Findlay recalled. ''The way they looked was terribly weird. It was what was ultimately called Futurist, I suppose, or New Romantic. They talked with a sincerity and a positiveness that I hadn't heard. They put on this tape of their demos. 'Chelsea Girl' got me cos it was obviously such a catchy tune, and I thought 'this band knows about

23

melody. This band can play a little bit'. 'Chelsea Girl' even had a classic little guitar solo in it. It had all the ingredients for a pop single, but that's not enough.

"But then 'Pleasantly Disturbed' came on, and the guy's playing a violin! I mean, how dare this new breed of musician be playing a violin? That's pomp rock, is it not? I thought it was stunningly good."

CHAPTER 3

Bruce went to see the band, encouraged by a hysterical report of their live shows from his assistant Brian Hogg, who also reviewed them for the Bruce's Records newsletter, *Cripes*. Findlay was duly converted to the Minds' cause.

"There they were in Glasgow, which is a notoriously heavy city, in the middle of the punk boom. It was still 'one two three four', Scots guys singing with Cockney accents and looking like Johnny Rotten. And there were Simple Minds in a tiny wee pub with 150 people, not big enough to swing a cat, with a girl working the lights and a guy doing sound. It looked so pompous in a way, and Jim was singing like he was onstage at the Apollo. The audience were *that* close to him but he was still able to create that distance. It seemed so pretentious and it was *fabulous*. I was totally blown away, I'd never seen anything like it in my life. They had so many interesting riffs in one song, and any one of them could be the classic riff in any song. Particularly in those days, they just washed over you in wave upon wave . . . fabulous."

In fact Bruce liked them so much that he more or less moved out of Edinburgh and moved in with Brian McGee in Glasgow. His friends from the chic Edinburgh social circuit were not slow to point out that Bruce was in danger of making a fool of himself, hanging about with a bunch of youths in make-up who not only called themselves a stupid name but were almost young enough to be his kids. Luckily for him, Findlay didn't listen.

"I'd just separated from my wife at that point, so I was a bachelor again. I just moved in with the band and became their . . . *friend*. I was much older than they were, but nevertheless we hit it off. I felt like a 19-year-old with Simple Minds – I knew I wasn't, but I felt that spirit."

McGee added, "Bruce stayed in my house for three months before we even decided to go ahead with him, coming back and forward to Glasgow from Edinburgh solidly. We just kept going and going, staying at my house, talking about what we wanted to do, getting to know each other. Then we said 'right, let's go' – it was really worth it. We never took any chances, even when Simple Minds was first started."

The Minds' reputation as a live act continued to grow, fuelled by the group's penchant for bizarre presentation. Kerr, once known as "Gentleman Jim" on the Toryglen council estate because he was polite to everyone and never got his clothes dirty like his younger brother Paul, was transformed onstage from his shy, stammering self into a performer of breathtaking cheek and ambition. Derek Forbes used to wear panda-like eye make-up, girls' sandals like the New York Dolls, and his grandmother's lurex top.

"Aye, you could see something happening," Forbes reflected. "I thought Jim was great, I thought Charlie was great. And I'd never ever played with a keyboard player like Mick. I used anything we could get hold of for the bass, cos we never had the money at the time. I had this old white bass cabinet we called the Fridge. Simple Minds in the early days was pretty magical, to think back on it – maybe it wasn't if I'd seen them from the audience, but it was just like a small pub and you'd never ever seen bands with lights and all that and taking the time to put on a show. Everybody had make-up on, but I was the only blond in the band, wearing all this lurex and leopardskin."

Then there was Charlie Burchill, who couldn't be satisfied with just a guitar, as David Henderson remembered. "Charlie used to make guitars and violins out of orange boxes or something. He made this violin that was shaped like a Flying V guitar – it never really worked very well, but he actually got it to play a couple of times. I think it was seeing the Doctors Of Madness that made him want to use a violin. We were really lucky with support slots too, because we got people that Jim and

26

Charlie really liked, like the Doctors Of Madness and Ultravox early on, and then later on there was the tour with Magazine."

Gigs became increasingly frequent, as the Minds became known as the best band in the neighbourhood. "We got a few Glasgow support dates," said Kerr, "and if a band needed to fill a couple of hundred seats they'd put us in because we had a following." Inevitably they began to get gigs outside Glasgow, too. On one occasion, they went onstage at 7.30 p.m. in Glasgow supporting Siouxsie and the Banshees, then dashed offstage, packed up their gear, drove to Edinburgh and supported Beatles-copyists the Pleasers the same night.

Their schedule began to create problems. Mick MacNeil's engineering apprenticeship, for example, became increasingly difficult to maintain as a result of the band's strenuous late nights. But by now, Mick had become confident enough about his future with the group to realize what his priorities were.

"Mick got this letter to send to his boss from Bruce," Kerr recalled, "and it was pure bullshit. It said 'this lad is involved in a band that could potentially be the business, so if he's late getting into work don't hassle him too much'. Apparently Mick was an amazing apprentice as well.

"One night we went to Aberdeen to support the Stranglers. The Skids were meant to be playing, and we went on and nobody had announced that the Skids wouldn't be there and they were all yelling 'Skiiiiids!' Nobody knew who we were and it was all just booing at the start, but by the end we got a really great reaction. We got back to Glasgow about half-seven in the morning, and Mick got into work about eight – fuckin' brain damage. I remember him saying that he never had any arguments with his boss, but after that night with the Stranglers he went into the toilet to have a cigarette and fell asleep for three hours. His boss gave him a hard time for the first time ever, and also for the first time Mick just told him to get fucked. We'd gone down amazingly onstage, and I think that must have given Mick a bit of bravado. Something had happened to his leg as well, and he'd had to go onstage on crutches."

But while there was no doubting the band's strength and increasing pulling-power, nobody was sure what was supposed

27

to happen next. Though Findlay's Zoom operation was funded by Arista, his budget wasn't big enough, as he saw it, to give the band the kind of backing they deserved. Neither Cranna nor Findlay was officially the group's manager, and the Minds themselves were turning a blind eye to a low murmur of record company interest. But Findlay kept raving about the Minds to Arista, and eventually the company's managing director, Charles Levison, and A&R man, Ben Edmunds, travelled up to Dunfermline to see them play live.

Arista had Lou Reed and Patti Smith on their roster, but any hipness reflected by these names was more than outweighed by label-mates like Barry Manilow, Showaddywaddy and pomp-rockist Alan Parsons. Nonetheless Levison was impressed with the Minds, and made Findlay an offer which it seemed foolish to refuse (Bruce having become the group's full-time spokesman by now, if not actually their manager). Arista would fund Findlay to sign Simple Minds to Zoom, thus apparently giving the band small-label independence coupled with the marketing and distribution clout of a major label.

This, remember, was 1978, the aftermath of punk, when major record companies were by definition evil capitalists solely concerned to exploit the honest working musician. Malcolm McLaren had purported to take the music business for a ride and to expose the Great Rock 'n' Roll Swindle, craftily turning the unremarkable notion that big business can be relied upon to crush the unwary into big bucks for himself. Independent labels were supposed to represent an ideal of low running costs, complete artistic licence and even-handed profit sharing. Unfortunately, this arrangement rarely worked out in the long run, and the Zoom/Arista tie-up was a compromise which was doomed from the very beginning.

"Forget it!" Bruce remembers. "They'd have been better being either independent or signing direct to a major, because what Arista did was bury Zoom. Everyone talked about Arista signing Simple Minds, it just looked so pathetic, it looked like a set-up."

At the time, though, the deal seemed like a triumph. Even in these early days, Simple Minds presented an unyielding façade when it came to business decisions and career prospects. Kerr:

"We got the deal with Arista, but we had good business sense because we just asked the absolutely logical questions, instead of trying to be clever. We never had any management when we signed the deal, it was a trial period with Bruce. I remember the first time Bruce took us out, he took us to this hamburger place in Glasgow and none of us took anything to eat so we wouldn't be in debt.

"Bruce was sitting there eating his meal and we were sitting there with glasses of water and things. We said 'we need a 3,000-watt PA system' and he was going 'what!' because at the time bands having their own PAs wasn't done. We said, 'well, we need it, and it can't be charged against royalties, and we need lights as well.' It was great, we got them too."

The band's relationship with Arista would prove to be full of frustration and misunderstandings, but the label at least had the sense to back the band's own wishes and contact John Leckie to work with them as the producer of their first album. Leckie was a thoughtful and rather ascetic figure, who could combine a high degree of technical know-how with an almost spiritual approach to music-making. Intuitively, Simple Minds had hit upon a man who would be able to cope with their occasionally wild impetuousness while making the most of their musical ideas.

Leckie could list some impeccable credentials. As an engineer at Abbey Road studios, he'd worked with Phil Spector on the Beatles' troublesome *Let It Be* project and then on George Harrison's marathon triple album, *All Things Must Pass*. Leckie learned much from watching the great Spector at close quarters (this was, after all, the man who invented the Wall of Sound and applied it to sixties classics like 'River Deep, Mountain High'). As a producer himself, Leckie had collaborated with some of the Minds' favourite artists like XTC, the Doctors Of Madness, and Magazine, for whom he produced the *Real Life* LP, as well as producing the first and very wonderful single by Public Image Ltd. He felt an immediate sympathy with the band.

"Arista phoned me up," said Leckie, "said they'd signed this band Simple Minds who I hadn't heard of at all, and sent me the demo tapes. I thought they were amazing. I said yes, I'll do it, definitely. Me and Ben Edmunds went up to the Dundee

29

Technical College Christmas dance, it was just before Christmas 1978. There were two separate gigs going on in the same college and everyone was pissed. There was Supercharge and Simple Minds and some dreadful Beatles impersonators.

"I thought Simple Minds were so mysterious, they were so kind of eerie. With Jim, there was a great kind of . . . not nervousness, it was more theatrical – it was sinister, but at the same time there was this kind of warmth. It was just a really good atmosphere, seeing them as basic and raw as they were, doing all those early songs."

Simple Minds were paid £75 for their performance, quite a generous fee by their standards at that time, but the drinks were on the record company that night. Leckie was surprised to find that Kerr and Burchill had been doing their homework on him.

"Jim was really nervous, and in those days he was much more kind of stuttery and things, but you knew he had something going on in his head, he just had a bit of a problem putting it out. So he really surprised me when I first met him, because the first thing he said to me was, 'Are you the John Leckie who produced the Doctors Of Madness?' Just before the Doctors split up, Jim and Charlie had hitched from Glasgow to Newcastle to see the Doctors play one of their last gigs, and spent the night sleeping in a half-built shop. All they wanted to know about was the Doctors, what they were like and all this. So that's how I met them."

On 27 January 1979, Simple Minds began recording their first album at Farmyard Studios in Amersham. "They were really knocked out to hear themselves," said Leckie, "and the whole process of recording. Everyone was pretty nervous. You're always nervous the first time you meet musicians, especially with material that you don't really know."

Life In A Day was finished by early March, with the title track released as a single at the end of the same month. The album followed in mid-April. The tracks were felt to be unsatisfactory at the time by almost everybody except John Leckie and Arista, though in retrospect this seems a harsh judgment. Nobody in their right mind would choose to hear 'Sad Affair' again, but the LP sounds fresh and energetic, and despite some ingredients derived from the obvious people like Roxy and Bowie it contains several potent songs. 'Life In A Day' and 'Chelsea Girl' are self-evidently strong, while the eight-minute mock-orchestral epic, 'Pleasantly Disturbed', features precocious performances from Burchill on thundery guitar and screeching violin. There was plenty of drive emanating from Forbes and McGee too, a bass and drums team which any number of personnel changes in later years could never quite equal for straightforward punch.

" 'Pleasantly Disturbed' is still probably one of the only tracks that I can hear now and understand that it was a thing we were getting right," said Charlie Burchill later. "There was another song that hearing it back sounds a bit daft, but for some reason I've always had this belief in 'All For You'. It was a bit heavy and all that, but I remember when we got it together it was the first spark of us really using harmony – as opposed to using conventional chords we were using ninths, you know. And it was the first sort of experiment in that field we ever did."

Perhaps the most obvious thing about *Life* is the way it adheres rigidly to conventional song structure, something the group would veer drastically away from on their next couple of releases. All songs are credited to Burchill and Kerr, and, as Leckie pointed out, it was virtually folk music – there's hardly anything here you couldn't sit down and play on an acoustic guitar.

Kerr freely acknowledged a debt to Lou Reed. "The riff for 'Chelsea Girl' was nicked off a Lou Reed song from *Rock 'n' Roll Heart* called 'Temporary Thing'," he revealed. "We could never seem to get a good riff of our own so we had to rip off somebody else's – I mean, every song in the world's a Velvets riff." But the song wasn't about Nico and New York, as you might have assumed. "I think it was much more about Jean Shrimpton-type people. That glamour, but fatal, sorta thing."

The traditionally-built songs were heavily camouflaged, though. Burchill was everywhere on guitar, devising crunchy riffs which galloped through 'Wasteland' and 'Murder Story', applying a keen rhythmic edge to 'Sad Affair' and cranking up the powerchords on 'Chelsea Girl'. MacNeil, meanwhile, let fly on all kinds of keyboards. He has a stylish minor-key workout

31

on synth in the middle of 'Wasteland', does an efficient Eno-impression in 'No Cure', and pitted mock-baroque harpsichord trills against Burchill's bludgeoning chords in 'Chelsea Girl'.

Amazingly, when the compact disc reissue of the album was reviewed by a UK hi-fi magazine in 1987, the reviewer believed it to be the Minds' follow-up to *Once Upon A Time*. While noting similarities to Cockney Rebel and even T Rex, the writer welcomed the group's brave new change of direction and wished them well with it. So maybe technology doesn't move on that much, after all.

But the band didn't like the album at all. Leckie: "They always put down those early days, the first album, which I had a go at them about one time. I said, 'Don't put down the first album, it was still you, it was the way you were at the time, it was really good'." Later, Kerr would describe his reaction to the album as "like the sort of embarrassment you feel when you look at an old photo, but it's still you."

Ian Cranna was among many who felt the album did the band little justice. "That first album was such a disappointment really to me, because they were such a thrilling, exciting band to watch. They had such a sure-footed melodic touch and pace, and it was such an adrenalin rush to sit there and watch them. I think 'Someone' is the only track that comes anywhere near to capturing any of that on record. I always felt that something had been lost. I just wish that videos had been a bit more commonplace at the time. But I was quite relieved to find that Jim and the others were as disappointed with it as I was. I didn't like the idea of having to tell my favourite band that I didn't like their album."

Already, the best-laid marketing schemes began to go awry. It was clear to all parties that 'Chelsea Girl' was the song with the greatest chart potential, but the plan was to release 'Life In A Day' first as an appetite-whetter, then to deliver the knockout stroke with 'Chelsea Girl'. Inexplicably, while 'Life In A Day' reached 60-something, 'Chelsea Girl' simply disappeared without trace, and resisted all efforts to revive it.

"All they lived for at Arista was 'Chelsea Girl'," John Leckie reflects. "They wanted me to remix it for a 12-inch version, and

I couldn't really better the original, actually. I spent a day at Utopia studios mixing it again, then compared it to the original and the original was just so much better. I told Arista you couldn't extend it, it was all there. The band hate 'Chelsea Girl', they really do, and they wouldn't get behind it or promote it or really do anything for Arista re-releasing it."

There was some compensation in the fact that the album reached the bottom end of the Top 30, a respectable effort for a debut, but Arista's enthusiasm had already been dampened by the absence of a big hit single. However, there should have been considerable grounds for optimism. The Minds had set a precedent by being invited to perform on BBC TV's *Old Grey Whistle Test* without having a record released (though they would have a few days later). The programme had finally dumped "Whispering" Bob Harris as presenter, a man fond of soft rock, progressive-length guitar solos and shoulder-length hair, and had installed Anne Nightingale in his place. She herself hardly flaunted avant-garde tastes, but Simple Minds served very well as a symbol of a new sound and a new broom.

Then on 16 April 1979, they played at Malvern Winter Gardens on the first night of a 20-date British tour supporting Magazine. It was a perfect pairing, since Magazine embodied much of what Simple Minds aspired towards. They mixed imagination with technology, a sense of mystery with an aura of intellectualism, the best of the past with a view to a dazzling tomorrow.

"They created a technical intensity, a sublime tension unique to themselves," wrote Paul Morley about Magazine, "in much the same magical ways as groups like Roxy Music and the Velvet Underground." Indeed, these words could have been written about Simple Minds, whom Morley would also champion at length in the pages of the *NME*. Morley, who would later launch the ZTT label and be one of the guiding hands behind the Frankie Goes To Hollywood phenomenon, was exactly the kind of supporter the group needed. He commanded enough respect as a journalist and style-detector to confirm that the band were more than a flash in the pan, and to suggest that they merited serious attention.

Kerr would repay the compliment in an interview with the

New Zealand music paper *Rip It Up* in 1982. ''I think Morley is one of the few great Englishmen around,'' he said. ''Some of the things he's done in the past five years are as important as any band.''

But for the time being, the Minds were finding out what life as a support band felt like. Although they were only paid a ludicrous £50 per night on the tour (a time-honoured gesture from concert promoter to support band), Simple Minds were able to warm themselves with the reflection that while their album had jumped straight into the chart, Magazine's *Secondhand Daylight* was floundering badly.

The tour proved to be an instructive experience for Jim Kerr, though not in the ways he'd anticipated. Before, he'd been somewhat in awe of Howard Devoto and the highbrow air the members of Magazine managed to give off, but already experience had begun to clear the stars out of his eyes. Deep down, Kerr knew that Simple Minds already had it in them to outdistance most of their contemporaries.

CHAPTER 4

"We were a lot shyer then, on our first tour," Kerr said, looking back in 1983. "Howard Devoto and John McGeoch and all of them were like the London scene and we were just like lads from Glasgow who'd paid a fortune to get on the tour. But it was a great tour for us and we went down really well. It was our whole thing, it had been like 'get a deal, get a tour, it has to be with Magazine'. The halls were full, and it was just like a sort of privilege. I think anyone could have got the tour if they'd paid the money."

But disillusion subsequently set in, as Kerr's naivety was chipped away by what he saw around him. "I loved Magazine, I really did," Kerr said. "They were one of the first bands who could play, as well as coming out of the British punk thing. They could have everything that punk had, and so much more intelligence and wit and charisma and artistic sense.

"I first went to see them because I had a friend in the support band. They did a version of 'Goldfinger' – I don't know what I'd think of it now, but it was brilliant. And then in the last song, when Howard sang 'the light pours out of me', I just thought 'what a fucking thing to say! Just absolutely incredible!' We started to get the band together about two weeks after that.

"Then when we went on tour with Magazine I was really let down by them, cos I was thinking they'd be really inside what they were doing. But apart from Howard, the rest were just fucking dullheads, absolute wallies, unaware of the greatness they were part of. When I saw Howard he was never like a wee thin balding man, he was everything much more than that. But

35

just towards the end, you became aware that in every picture you saw of him there was a lightbulb above his head and stuff. Then you started to think, 'fucking hell, sure Howard.'"

The Magazine dates kicked Simple Minds off into what would be a year of virtually uninterrupted touring, apart from a few weeks spent recording a second album in August and September 1979 and a break around New Year, 1980. They played all over Britain, from Barbarella's in Birmingham to the Fusion club in Chesterfield and the Kirklevington Country Club. In London, they played well-attended shows at the Marquee, the Nashville and the Music Machine, where they were studied by celebrities like Gary Numan, Boomtown Rat Bob Geldof and The Jam's Paul Weller (though Weller would become one the band's pet hates in the fullness of time). They would visit most of the countries of Europe and play a couple of club dates in New York, and by December 1979 Jim Kerr would be all but flattened by exhaustion.

The English music press had been resistant to the Minds initially. Being London-based, the papers tended to react with scepticism to distant reports of provincial phenomena, as Ian Cranna discovered from behind his typewriter in Edinburgh. "You try and persuade the *NME* down there in London that this band they'd never heard of was worth all these column inches – it didn't mean a light to them, and I was only a freelance contributor, blah blah blah. An original review I wrote of them hung about for weeks and weeks before a very truncated version was finally published."

The Minds didn't go out of their way to ingratiate themselves with the press. Moreover, talking about a group like Genesis as a source of inspiration was tantamount to treason in the eyes of the custodians of cool down in London.

"There was this London hipness thing, I think," said Cranna. "Once a word like 'Genesis' is dead, people are much too afraid to stand up and say, 'Well, I used to really like Genesis, they were a band who used to mean something, who *did* have inspiration in those days and did represent an alternative to mindless pap'. The Minds weren't afraid to admit it, being typically forthright Glaswegians, and they got slagged by

36

people who said Genesis were as dead as a doornail. There was also the thing of them growing up in Glasgow and staying up in Glasgow. They weren't on the machine in London, where I think there is a subconscious thing, especially in the likes of the *NME* where a band has to get a stamp of approval at a fairly early stage. Otherwise it's sort of, 'Who are these? Where did they come from?' I don't know if they feel some sort of threat, or something."

Ironically, it was in the *NME* that Tony Stewart wrote by far the most enthusiastic review of *Life In A Day*, hailing the band as a signpost for a new musical direction for the eighties, but elsewhere reaction to the first album had been mixed. Nevertheless, it was beginning to dawn on some journalists that this was a band with growth potential. With an album in the charts and their tally of gigs mounting rapidly, their stock had risen, and they were now able to command £300 or more per show. It still didn't pay the bills.

The Minds' treadmill of touring, broken only by recording sessions, was to set the pattern for coming years. The group's virtual obsession with motion and travel would build them a firm, loyal audience in numerous countries and would nourish their music in many ways, but would also impose severe physical and emotional strain. But, at the time, the world was still a mysterious and unconquered place to them, despite Kerr and Burchill's hitchhiking trips around Europe between leaving school and forming the band.

"Ten years ago we ran away from something, I think," says Kerr now, "when we decided to get a band together. Other bands would probably argue, but that was our motivation, it was definitely escape into our own world. Live your own hours. Play where you want to play. And I totally advocate it – it's great, it's incredible."

Bruce Findlay at last became the group's full-time manager, which was a source of some pride and considerable worry to him. It provoked a certain prickliness between Findlay and Ian Cranna, too, since the group's choice of managers was finally decided one uncomfortable night at the Caledonian Hotel in Edinburgh. Bruce will talk until the cows come home and will then talk to the cows, while Cranna is altogether quieter and more scholarly. He was out-ranted on the night, and was too introverted to mount an effective challenge to Findlay's confident display.

"We all went to the pub later and we were really getting annoyed at Ian for not having said anything," Jane Henderson remembered. "I think Ian felt bad, as if the group didn't have any confidence in him or should have stood up for him, or something. But he wasn't forceful at all and he didn't really make any comment."

Unremarkably, Cranna harbours considerable scepticism about Findlay. "The diplomatic way of putting it would be that Bruce takes his direction from Jim," he said. "It was obvious even from the early days that Jim was the one who really counted. I think the rest of the band were happy to go along with what Jim would say or do because he had such a clear vision, and also he was motivated in a way that they are not when it comes to business. Like, Mick is such a nice guy, but he's pure musician in that he's not particularly interested in the business side or the packaging side. He's happy to leave that to Jim, as were the rest, I think. I think the period at Arista is really down to Bruce's lack of foresight, just general weak management, really, which is why the group spent so long in the wilderness."

As for Findlay, he won't be drawn into a slanging match. "Ian was a wee bit posh for me, a wee bit reserved, we wouldn't go and get bevvied together and things. But I really like him." Meanwhile, Findlay's record shops had now been taken over by the Guinness brewery group. "I had bosses again. They were well pissed off with me driving around the country with this weird group of little faggots, and pretending to be a pop group manager with a record label."

Something had to go, so it was the record shops. "I knew I was the right side of forty to make the sort of decision which seemed stupid to everybody else," said Bruce. "It was the last time older people would say to me, 'When are you gonna grow up?' Because they'd all be dead the next time, and I would be one of the older people myself. It was the last chance I had to make a wild decision, and I gave up an awful lot to do it." After Bruce bailed out of the record retailing business, his brother Brian

38

converted the original Bruce's Records Shop in Rose Street, Edinburgh, into a successful delicatessen.

The bond between Findlay and the band was as much emotional as practical. Both parties would acknowledge that Bruce had shortcomings as a manager, but his loyalty and enthusiasm for the Minds were unquestionable.

Jim Kerr: "It's not like Malcolm McLaren or Brian Epstein or anything. Bruce doesn't make any decision without us being involved. He's good like that, and he also knows that to get the best out of us we've got to know all the conditions. I think Bruce is the best manager we could have. He just loves the band, it's all he talks about. The band was his breadline, but we didn't believe that. We thought, 'Oh, he's got more money in the bank from Bruce's Records, the band is just a whim.' But you never get him in a bad mood, he's always like the same thing, sort of busy and a bit mad, really."

Brian McGee: "Bruce isn't the best manager in the world, you know, he's clumsy in a lot of ways and very weak in a lot of ways an' all, but he deserves to be where he is now because of what he's done in the past. Bruce is like my dad, that's the way he was to me. He's a fatherly figure among the band. Although sometimes he was treated like shit."

Simple Minds were by no means a simple proposition to work with. Alongside their belligerent sense of mission, they could be stubborn, unreasonable and, at times, self-destructive. If Arista had little understanding of the group, the group made little or no effort to explain themselves, as Jane Henderson recollects.

"I suppose Arista did try, but they didn't get much help from Jim and Charlie because they said 'it should be apparent in the music', and they were quite precious about the songs and things which were demanded of them. They were also quite difficult when Arista wanted demos of the songs for the first album before it was recorded. They didn't feel there was anyone in the company who could advise them how to write songs."

Arista's efforts to shape or promote the band were invariably disastrously misguided. Jane Henderson: "I'd done these posters of Jim's head with red eyes on them – they got these things all printed up and put them up in London, then they were asking

Jim to get red contact lenses to wear on stage, and they wanted to send him to mime school with Lindsay Kemp because they thought maybe that's what he wanted. The only way Arista seemed able to work was if they could find a gimmick to be latched on to the band."

If the company had been expecting further potential hit singles from the Minds' second album, they were in for a shock. *Real To Real Cacophony* was recorded over five weeks at Rockfield Studios in Monmouthshire, once again with John Leckie at the controls. This time, the group were determined to give Arista no opportunity to interfere whatsoever, and, as far as possible, the studios were declared off limits to everybody but the band.

"Arista was always a bit tricky and the band never really liked 'em at all," said Leckie. "They could never see the reason why these groovy record biz A&R people would come up to the studio or come to the gigs and say 'hi, I'm your A&R man, great gig chaps' and all this sort of thing. The band just hated all that."

This much became evident, particularly to Arista's new head of A&R, the fantastically-named Tarquin Gotch. Tarquin drove down to Rockfield to see how the Minds were getting on with *Real To Real*. The group were automatically suspicious of anybody from the record company, and had taken a particular dislike to the unfortunate Tarquin when he'd had the cheek to suggest ideas for the artwork for *Real To Real*. He became the focus for much collective frustration. The following morning, Gotch got up to find that his plush company car had been thickly coated with a stomach-turning mixture of eggs, Domestos bleach, instant mashed potato and other commodities too vile to mention. Moreover, the sun was shining brightly and had baked the mixture irrevocably and ruinously onto the vehicle. The culprits were never apprehended, but Tarquin was reasonably confident he knew who'd done it.

As it happened, David Bowie was at Rockfield at the same time as the Minds, helping his old chum Iggy Pop to record his album *Soldier*. Bowie's work and his manipulation of image had already been a major source of inspiration for the members of Simple Minds. His collaborations with the drug-raddled Iggy on

Raw Power, *The Idiot* and *Lust For Life* had helped Pop to claw himself back from the brink of self-annihilation so that he, too, could begin to fulfil his considerable potential. Both men were heroes, in varying degrees. The Minds were awestruck.

They immediately decided they wanted Bowie to play a bit of saxophone on *Real To Real*, but were shy of asking him. The no-nonsense Forbes, who was always enough of a groupie to tackle any celebrity he happened to come across, whether it was Lulu or Paul McCartney, was detailed to seek out the great man and put the question. Forbes made it as far as the next-door studio but then faltered. He sat nervously listening to playbacks of Pop's material, and couldn't pluck up the courage to ask Bowie. Forbes went back to get Kerr for some moral support, but Bowie, quick-witted as ever, was too sharp for them. Before they'd got a word in, he said "Can you sing?", gave them some headphones, and got them singing backing vocals for 'Play It Safe'.

Members of the Minds sang on several more of Pop's tracks, but the presence of greatness next door didn't prevent them from wrapping up *Real To Real* in good time. It was released in November 1979, and had been conceived as the complete antithesis of *Life In A Day*. Where the first album had cut-and-dried tunes, *Real To Real* had experimental noise and thundering bass riffs. *Life In A Day* was patently derivative, but large chunks of its successor sounded like nothing on earth. Any attempts to pigeonhole them as a pop group now lay in ruins.

The band loved it, and still do. Mick MacNeil: "There's a lot on *Real To Real*, and it's all really good. The reason it's got so many tracks on it is because the ideas hadn't had enough time to develop, because there *weren't* really any ideas. It was really, really basic. We went into the studio with pieces and patches and couldn't quite get them to fit together to make one thing, even though the album was much more one thing than any of them. It's just a load of wee ideas and we got it all on tape, and it's all on the record."

Jim Kerr: "*Real To Real* was laughing at ourselves, which I think is healthy, particularly with our sort of music where we're leaving ourselves open maybe to accusations of having pretensions beyond our station. Two months after *Life In A Day* came out we were really embarrassed by it. It was very, very poppy and we recognized that we were drowned in influence. We had to try and get our own sound, a sound which was much more us. We had to stop messing about.

"So we were getting really interested in sounds at that stage, in writing actual songs, and we had all these backing tracks that we just worked on in a different way, with all these different sounds going in and coming through. And 'Cacophony' just summed up the outcome."

The Minds went into the studio with only three or four songs written. "I often tell people that we went in to do *Real To Real* with nothing written at all," Leckie remembers. "Bruce and myself convinced the record company that we didn't need to do demos, we were going to come out with a hit album and just trust us to do it. I went to see them play some gigs, but we never actually rehearsed for the sessions.

"We sat down in the studio on the first evening and I said, 'What have you got?' I knew they had 'Premonition', because they'd been playing it live. They had 'Carnival' – which was going to be a single but never was – and 'Real To Real' was written. But other than that, Mick just had a few tunes on the synth and that's all we went in with. 'Changeling' was just a riff – one of Derek's, I think."

Fortunately, Leckie's imagination and willingness to fly by the seat of his pants fitted in perfectly with the group's attitude. There was a collective awareness that Simple Minds had to prove to all and sundry that they were a different proposition to the power-pop faddists or 2-Tone bandwaggoners then clogging the clubs and the charts. Their arrogance and single-mindedness, they knew, could only be justified by some positive results. They would just have to put their money where their mouths were.

Real To Real was so strange and so strong that *Life In A Day* might never have happened. The group were clearly developing a shaping intelligence, backed up with a flair for finding unusual sounds with which to express their teeming ideas. A few days before the sessions began, Burchill had bought himself a saxophone, and though he'd never tried to play the instrument before, he made enough progress with it to play it on the album (so they didn't need David Bowie after all). It demanded a certain type of confidence, too, to produce a record so full of false trails and startling squibs of imagination without feeling the need to clean them up and round them off.

The album's first side, in particular, was a collection of strange semi-realized ideas. 'Citizen' sounded like something from the TV series *The Prisoner*, with its unspecified accusations and mentions of "crimes against the state". "I still really like 'Citizen'," said Charlie Burchill. "I think the drum sounds on it are brilliant and I think the vocal's great."

'Carnival' extended the notion of the band cavorting on stolen instruments in a haunted fairground with which 'Real To Real' itself had opened the album. Child-like riffs and melodies scampered among McGee's tough drumbeats and Forbes' dense bass. There were also throwaway displays of musical expertise, like the crafty shifts between 3/4 and 4/4 time in 'Naked Eye'.

'Cacophony' was little more than a splintered guitar riff punctuated by off-colour synth embellishments, a kind of prototype for 'Scar' which closes the album. 'Veldt', on the other hand, chucked all ideas about structure down the sink. Beginning with a distant tribal drumbeat, it grew steadily into a maelstrom of sound textures and jungle-line roars and chirrups, including Derek Forbes' celebrated impersonation of a chimp.

John Leckie remembered how 'Veldt' came to be written, or created. "It came about from a discussion on how you write a song. Musicians write songs one way, but from a musical point of view, and I'm not really a musician. And Jim's not a musician. Me, Jim and Charlie were saying, 'How do you write a song?' and we kind of got into approaching it like you would write a film. We said, 'well, a song has an atmosphere, if you're not going to write a conventional song that has a melody'. What came out in the end was the idea, the picture, and 'Veldt' was really a picture.

"It went through all sorts of different things. There was probably something in the news about South Africa or Zimbabwe – the veldt is the South African prairie, Jim had

43

remembered the word from school and wanted to know what it was. There's all that clashing sound too, that *kssssh* sound that comes in at the end that really sounds like swords clashing. And there's voices, Jim and Derek trying to be aborigines or something."

Mick MacNeil recalled a different sort of input that helped them record 'Veldt'. "There was this story by Ray Bradbury, the science fiction writer. It was about this futuristic family living in a house and they had this room with video-walls in it. You could programme it a certain way so you were actually there, wherever you wanted to go in the world. The kids kept going to Africa, and their mum and dad didn't think it was a good idea that they kept going there, but the machine started getting a bit dodgy when they went anywhere else. Their dad got the machine switched off and the kids were really pissed off. Then they got him to go into the room, locked him in, switched the machine on and the lions ate him. So we got this jungly beat with all these space noises. It was great fun doing it, and it was great how we got away with it."

The second side of *Real To Real* was more structured and sharply focused. It kicked off with 'Premonition', an exhilarating slab of hard rock powered by Forbes' looming riff and another of Burchill's powerchord exercises. The song would become a stage favourite for years, and suggested that the Minds could have had a profitable career in Kerrang! country if they'd had the inclination. The song's oppressive atmosphere and use of repetition to build momentum also hinted at the direction they'd take on *Empires And Dance* the following year. 'Changeling', again, circled around a brutal, stalking beat and McGee's thwacking percussion, while 'Calling Your Name' was a chunk of heavy pop which picked up the pace somewhat.

Another pointer to future developments was 'Film Theme', the first in a series of Simple Minds instrumentals and an early sign of the group's frequently-expressed interest in making music to go with film. It had been dreamed up by Mick and Charlie, who were becoming the chief ideas-factory for the band's music. Starting from a simple descending motif, 'Film Theme' moved through increasingly elaborate variations before fading discreetly into the distance. Maybe it was 'Film Theme' that prompted a French TV crew to consider using music from *Real To Real* as a soundtrack for a documentary they were making about film director Bertrand Tavernier, though the project eventually came to nothing. The fusion of music and film would benefit both parties in the fullness of time, though. Tavernier would go on to make *Round Midnight*, his requiem for the jazz life, while the movie *The Breakfast Club* eventually gave Simple Minds their first shot at a film soundtrack as well as their breakthrough hit record.

CHAPTER 5

By its nature, *Real To Real* was guaranteed to upset Arista. *Life In A Day* had suggested a group with breezy commercial instincts, perfectly happy to play along with the kind of sounds that dominated the charts. *Real To Real* gave Arista that sinking feeling associated with words like "art". The record company wanted a Police, or would probably have settled for a successful bunch of Mod revivalists, of the kind they were already signing in the shape of Secret Affair. Instead it looked as though they were lumbered with a Magazine, a group with lots of credibility who couldn't, or wouldn't, write hits.

"When we took the second album into Charles Levison's office on the day we finished it, we realized they were expecting it to be just like the first," said Kerr. "We played a tape of it to him, there was a lengthy silence and he said, 'I'll have to play it to the rest of the company'."

The record company were at a loss. No particular promotional effort was put behind *Real To Real*, which fared less well than *Life In A Day*. 'Changeling' was released as a single but flopped, Levison apparently admitting to Kerr a few weeks later that the company knew it would never be a hit anyway. With so fatalistic an attitude prevalent at the company which held the strings to their future, morale within the group inevitably began to wilt somewhat.

For the time being, they kept plugging away on the live circuit. They ended 1979 with a show at Glasgow Technical College, where they played 'In Your Room' onstage for the first time, having written it for a recording session for John Peel's

46

Radio 1 programme the week before. In March 1980 they set off for Germany and several weeks of European dates, but by the time they returned to the UK they'd parted company with David Henderson, who'd been doing their sound as well as acting as road manager.

After an ugly public showdown, he'd been ousted by Billy Worton, an experienced sound engineer who'd been brought in by the management, although the Minds themselves felt that David should have stood his ground and fought to retain his position. Kerr, in particular, saw Henderson's submissive approach as evidence that he'd lost faith in Simple Minds, something the band members always found extremely difficult to forgive. As they saw it, it was sheer faith and determination that was driving them, and anyone who broke ranks had also transgressed a crucial unwritten law.

But, not unlike Ian Cranna, David was a fairly quiet character who wasn't accustomed to aggressive displays of self-assertion. He became the first casualty of Simple Minds' slow and painful progress towards international status and a more conventionally "professional" approach. He went on to run a rehearsal and recording studio in Glasgow called the Hellfire Club, and also became involved in managing a number of local groups.

That still left his sister Jane looking after the stage lighting. She'd never been entirely comfortable with the group's womanizing and all-boys-together behaviour on tour, though she was shielded somewhat by being romantically involved with Kerr. On one occasion in Germany, four of the group managed to get themselves infected by the same girl. As she tried to board their bus to travel to the next gig, Brian McGee flung her bags into the road, locked the bus and drove off, leaving her stranded.

Jane recalled: "They would stop in a service station in Germany or something and they would go straight for the pornographic magazines, and they'd run up and show me – 'what do you think of that one?' kind of thing, to shock me. But they would sort of look after me – you end up being a kind of sister to them all. I was treated really, really well by the band. A lot of girls are quite vicious, in a way, when they're trying to get to the band, but I just tended to keep out of the way of them. The

47

band were really chauvinistic, though, and most of the girls never hung around for more than a night or two."

The group toured solidly until May, rattling across Europe for a punishing string of one-nighters in Germany, France, Belgium and Holland. At a mini-festival at the Pavillion Baltard in Paris, the Minds had a furious argument with the Rezillos about who should top the bill, and upset the promoter and French band Marquis De Sade. The promoter slagged them off for being a "difficult English band", prompting Kerr to swot up enough French to tell the crowd that *"nous sommes Ecossais"* ("we're Scottish"). The Minds were joined onstage by Richard Jobson for an encore of Iggy Pop's 'Sister Midnight', and rumour had it that following threats from some of the more violent French punks in the crowd, at least a couple of the Minds went onstage with knives hidden up their sleeves.

For all their aloofness and faintly cerebral aura, Simple Minds were Glaswegians through and through, not to be tangled with lightly. Back at London's Marquee in December, Kerr had responded to having glasses thrown at him by laying somebody's head open with his mike stand. On more than one occasion, too, Charlie Burchill had leapt offstage to sort out troublesome punters, not the kind of behaviour you'd expect from the small and unfailingly cheerful guitarist.

In the midst of this European trek, the Minds also played a few dates supporting Gary Numan, robot king of electro-disco. Following his first hit with Tubeway Army, 'Are "Friends" Electric?', Numan had struck out on a solo career, and had subsequently inflicted songs like 'Cars' and 'We Are Glass' on a curiously gullible public. Numan's success was based on making simplistic replicas of the sort of music David Bowie had been producing on albums like *Heroes* and *Lodger*, converting Bowie's unsettling innovations into a Space Invader pop easily sucked into the charts. Numan's music also suggested that he'd made the acquaintance of some of the German electronic groups, like Neu and Kraftwerk, though his own work was conspicuous by its blank humourlessness and technological self-importance.

But it was grist to Simple Minds' creative mill. During this intense period of travel, they soaked up people, news, sounds, politics and headlines like a workaholic team of documentary-makers. At a gig at Berlin's Kant-Kino club, Kerr was impressed when he heard the Minds' song 'Premonition' easily holding its own alongside more established, respected names like Bowie, Donna Summer or Talking Heads. The moment inspired a piece named after the club for the forthcoming *Empires And Dance* album.

During this period, terrorist activity was reminding mainland Europe of what it feels like to live in Belfast or Beirut. It was impossible to ignore the police operation sweeping across the continent, a surveillance and dragnet exercise set against a back-drop of rising hysteria. Police with machine-pistols guarded airports and railway stations, and every border crossing cranked the tension a little higher as black-caped gendarmes or Staats-polizei searched the band's bus and checked passports. For the band, though, it was still an adventure. They were constantly moving on, and didn't have to stick around to see the consequences of political and social upheaval. They could register the tension and suspicion without falling victim to it. And they could make music out of it. As Kerr would say later, it was a voyeuristic experience.

John Leckie described the spirit which fuelled the group in these exciting, disturbing days. "Simple Minds have retained this kind of . . . I hate to use the word 'schoolboy', but it's like a schoolboy comradeship. You can't break that down at all. Brian McGee was mad, an absolute loony. You could dare him to do anything – he didn't need daring, in fact. He was the only one in the band who could drive, he drove all around Europe because they were short of money and they had this European tour. There'd be the roadies in one van and he'd be driving the band and the gear. You know, find a gig somewhere in Germany or France, park the van, the roadies would unload his kit, he'd play the drums and then drive off to the hotel. It was just budget, really.

"We were driving around Edinburgh once and McGee had a water pistol, driving up to bus queues and squirting everybody, smacking people round the head. People would be waiting to cross the road and he'd go really slowly. The people would start to cross the road, then he'd go a little bit further, then they'd step back and as he drove past them he'd smack them on the head. Totally childish!"

But if their behaviour could be wilfully idiotic (was it really true that Kerr laid in a huge supply of shoes to throw at hotel chambermaids who woke him up too early?), the group's music was developing at cracking speed. Seeing the success of an artist like Gary Numan, whose hits were built on the cold, glittering surfaces now easily available from the ever-expanding range of synthesizers and other electronic instruments, made them realize how rich and complex their own music was becoming. The Minds, too, were learning to admire the German electronic groups who had quietly been letting their music mature since the mid-seventies, like Kraftwerk in their Dusseldorf lair, Neu, or another little-acknowledged unit called La Dusseldorf, of whom Brian McGee was especially fond.

Burchill: "The track 'Today I Died Again' from *Empires*, that was when we were listening to Neu, the German band. It was a pure accident that we happened to hear them, cos this German bird that we know gave Jim a Neu album and Jim was playing it to see what it was like. At that time I was just getting into the saxophone, and every five minutes this big drone would come in with the sax, and the guitar was all just jangle. There wasn't any definite musical content in it, yet you didn't have to justify it, it was like the only way they knew how to do something without contriving it. Instead of trying to fake it up they were just going for it. That's why I liked 'Today I Died Again', cos it's dead like Neu in a lot of ways, though it's more refined than the way they would sound."

The European approach to music also had an impact on Kerr, despite his non-musician credentials. "We used to hitch-hike in Europe. We knew the place before joining the group. We liked groups liked Neu and Dusseldorf and Can, all of whom are influenced by the Velvet Underground. You get a black kind of bassline, then these high notes with sweet melodies for the guitar – little chimes. We've always found them more innova-tive. The Americans are good at doing something well – the best funk people are in America. But it's not what you necessarily want. You can use that in a different context. The Europeans have got a much better suss for keyboards and sounds, it's very mature."

Kerr could never come to grips with the way Europe was riven by so many political and ideological divisions. It seemed easy for Simple Minds to drive where they wanted across the continent, yet in reality vast barriers criss-crossed Europe like unseen force-fields.

"I get so bitter about Europe being cut up, it absolutely infuriates me," he said. "We were in Helsinki and it's forty miles from the Russian border, and yet you and I can't go there. I was talking to someone the other night and his mother's East German and his father's Russian, and Europe's such a hotch-potch and so much travelling has been done over the years, you don't know what blood cells you've got in you. When I was in Ireland I thought I was Irish, and as it turns out I have got a lot of Irish in me. I've often thought about spending the first half of your life as a decadent Westerner and then for the other half just turning it round and going to Russia."

It was considerations like these which generated the music of *Empires And Dance*, the band's third album and a record which still stands as a milestone in Simple Minds' career. If there had been impressive moments on *Real To Real*, *Empires And Dance* presented a band who had suddenly taken a giant leap forward in creativity and maturity. *Empires* was a complete package in sound and vision, with even its experimental moments sub-sumed into a coherent whole.

Once again John Leckie was in charge, though he discovered later that at one point Arista had actually booked David Cunningham of the Flying Lizards to produce the album. But Leckie had, by now, become virtually the sixth member of the band, and his partnership with the Minds reached its fullest and most ambitious expression on *Empires*. Basic recording was again done down at Rockfield, then Leckie took the tapes to the Townhouse in London's Shepherd's Bush for mixing and additional overdubs. This time, the group came to the sessions with several songs which they'd been playing live, including 'In Your Room', 'This Fear Of Gods' and 'Capital City' (originally called 'Pulse') while they had also sketched out ideas for 'I Travel' and 'Celebrate'. They soon got into their recording stride, and new songs would often begin with Derek Forbes generating one of his thrusting basslines, as in the case of 'Today I Died Again'.

"We'd say 'give us a bassline, Derek'," Leckie remembered, "and he'd go dum-dubba-dubba-dum and we'd build on it from there. I think we all went through a kind of development stage together. I guess I kind of questioned – I guess *they* questioned – their ability. Derek was always The Musician. Mick was the kind of academic musician because he was the keyboards man, while Derek was the performing musician. He could play all the Beatles' songs on guitar, he could sit at the piano and play Mozart or something. He could do anything, he was great, a real performer.

"It's not really down to ability, it's down to doing your best, doing what you really can do, and I think that's what they did on those records with me – that's what they're still doing. I think they were criticized by people who said, 'Well they don't have any songs, they're not real songs, they're just sort of atmospheres and ideas, pieces put to music,' you know. But I don't think that really matters. It's a very old-fashioned way of looking at it."

CHAPTER 6

On *Empires*, the Minds brought their semi-mathematical approach to music to an early fruition. Several critics applied the easy tag of "disco" to the album, but they were merely checking a point of departure from which the music set out in all kinds of exploratory directions. Suddenly they'd found a voice which was distinctively theirs. You could still hear traces of the heavy rock-isms and rampant experimentalism of *Real To Real*, and the straightforward tunefulness of *Life In A Day* hadn't been entirely forgotten either, though the overall sound and sheer power might have been an entirely different band.

Comparisons were occasionally made with Gary Numan too, much to the chagrin of the Minds, and superficially you could see why. In a piece like 'Constantinople Line' the abruptly-stopping rhythm and dripping-tap synth sounded a little too much like moping Gary for comfort. The Minds shared with Numan an almost obsessive preoccupation with the cold mechanics of dance and with the hypnotic symmetry offered by the clean, clear circuitry of synthesizer and studio. The similarities ended there. Numan's music sounded simple because it was. For Simple Minds, on the other hand, their superficial logic was a means of expressing a rich confusion.

Empires began working on you right from the title and the cover artwork. The Parthenon fades into the dusk behind a statue of a military man, perhaps from the Great War. The group were already on the move, citizens of a recent crumbling empire taking in a tourist's-eye view of an ancient one. On the back of the sleeve, the group were overlaid in fuzzy monochrome, ghostly images in transit.

The opening track was the aptly-titled 'I Travel', and it instantly established radical changes in sound and approach. Forbes' bass was now mixed hard upfront, supplying a giant riff which suggested miles being swallowed whole as it galloped over countryside and down autobahns. It locked around the whirling rotorblade chop of MacNeil's synthesizers, which would be used throughout the album to generate stark, repeating patterns.

Overhead, Burchill had evolved a style of guitar-playing dimensions away from the conventional chords-and-lines approach he'd once adopted. Now, he deployed shrieks, wails, canny counterpoints and sly use of echo, backing up rhythms or commenting upon what Kerr or MacNeil were doing. Meanwhile, McGee's drums supplied a simple but massive backbeat. 'I Travel' blasted off *Empires* like a dawn assault by the Air Cavalry. It was the age of *Apocalypse Now*, worldwide terrorism and the dawn of the eighties. Simple Minds had assembled their own vocabulary to describe what they'd seen.

In 'This Fear Of Gods', saxophone and synthesizers jabbered like snake-charmers over the malignant throb of Forbes' bass to produce an effect of mounting terror. "Fear is fast I'm turning white boy," sang Kerr, sounding genuinely terrified, as though he were trapped in a dreamlike predicament of being unable to escape the horror pursuing him however fast he ran. Later, he would say, "Catholic faith is stamped a lot into you. Through fear, I think. I fear God. Even though you grow to see through it, you never escape, I think you're always oppressed by the fear of it."

The actual *sound* of the album was vital to its unsettling impact. The pendulum pulse of 'Capital City' was generated by apparently suspending McGee's drums in miles of open space, while MacNeil's playful keyboard tunes were scoured away by screams from Burchill's protesting guitar. "When we were doing 'Capital City', we recorded the backing track at five in the morning," Brian McGee remembered. "We were away, without even thinking about it, pushing each other on. I remember, when we finished it, feeling a pure 'thank fuck for that'. We all went to bed that morning and never got up until the next day.

54

With the sessions the band do, it was always keep going till you drop, you know. Got to get the best no matter how long it takes."

In 'Constantinople Line', Kerr sounded panicky and claustrophobic, as though he'd been locked in a wardrobe with only a microphone for company. On 'Celebrate', Leckie insisted that they use real handclaps instead of a machine like a Claptrap, to generate some tension between the metronomic stride of the backing track and the people who'd produced it.

"I always try and capture the organic thing of it," he explained. "I said, 'we're gonna do it live, it doesn't matter if we shout and scream, that's gonna be a part of it'. We'd all had a bit too much to drink and everyone was shouting and laughing. Then afterwards we thought, 'hang on a minute, maybe it's a bit too much'. There was too much shouting, it was over the words, so I'd have to drop in four or five handclaps and get the sound exactly the same, the same echo and everything. It took a long time."

On the other hand, gadgets sometimes unwittingly contributed new ideas. "We were doing an overdub with lots of effects and stuff," said Leckie, "and there was so much noise coming from Mick's effects and his speakers and his phaser that it sounded just like a film projector – you hear it at the beginning of 'Kant-Kino'. Someone said, 'Hey, we could use that for 'Thirty Frames A Second'', so I recorded, like, five minutes of it. It's just the noise that you would normally try to get rid of from the synths and the keyboards turned full up. We listened to this noise and there was a slow phase on it, just like a film projector going round.

"Charlie said, 'Oh, I can hear this little tune in there, it's going da da da-da, da dada da'. Then someone else would say, 'I can hear da da da, da da da'. It was all done by laying tape loops on top of each other, and they're completely out of sync. There was a tape loop of Charlie going dadadadada, it's a whole chord structure, then there's another loop of da da da on the piano. But they're not related; there's one loop on top of another and they're going at different speeds, so they don't actually follow each other at the same time."

This was the sort of applied randomness that Bowie and Eno had been experimenting with in the last few years, choosing a method of producing sound and then letting it evolve its own patterns and cross-references. Elsewhere on *Empires*, the same kind of thinking produced constantly intriguing results. Tracks seemed at first to be monotonous and unchanging, then movements and colouration began to reveal themselves.

In 'Celebrate', the stark basic beat was progressively diced, multiplied and darkened by squittering electronics, Burchill's dank guitar chording, shouts, handclaps and zooming bass licks. The song's rhythm demanded a double beat on the bass drum, which Brian McGee found difficult to maintain for six minutes, so Leckie put the drums on a tape loop. "So it started with a drum loop and Derek put the bass on, and the whole arrangement was laid down by Derek, really – and some of the gaps are Derek fumbling, making a mistake. He'd go, 'What comes next?' By the fade, the track resembled a huge piece of machinery running out of control, and the title had become more of a threat than an invitation.

In 'Capital City', guitars lapped against a heavy, striding beat constructed by Forbes and McGee, while Toytown motifs on organ and synth were by turns starkly pretty and insistently ominous as the focus shifted from hard to soft and back again. Kerr's lyric was as ominous and eerie as the music. In just a few short, repetitive lines he evoked a powerful sense of unfamiliarity, as if a space visitor was trying to describe his first impressions of earth – "I walk on by, where animals cry/To a city that they live on". The use of the word "on" instead of "in" was striking.

By the late summer of 1980, Arista were presented with one of the most powerful and original albums of the year. Yet again, they were unable to rise to the occasion, despite the fact that they'd heard demo tapes of 'I Travel', 'Celebrate' and 'Thirty Frames A Second' and so had some idea of what to expect.

By now, Bruce Findlay's Zoom label had in effect ceased to exist, since it had scored no hit records with its other acts and Arista had lost interest in funding it or distributing its releases. Seeing that the future with Arista was getting dimmer by the hour, Findlay had already attempted to find a home for Zoom with other major companies, and had approached Virgin. Richard Branson's crew might have been sufficiently tempted by the lure of Simple Minds to prise them away from Arista had they not already been committed to what they saw as a similar group, Magazine. According to Bruce, Virgin's reply was to the effect that "we're struggling to make Magazine a success and they're one of the most respected bands in Britain. What chance are we gonna have with Simple Minds?" For the time being, Bruce and his band were stuck with the situation, but *Empires* would bring it to a head.

Though the sleeve of *Empires And Dance* carried a Zoom logo, Simple Minds' original financial demands (lights, PA, crew, recording budget) had led Arista to sign them with a separate contract from Findlay's deal for Zoom. With Zoom, to all intents and purposes, defunct, the group found themselves bound to a company which simply had no comprehension of how best to market and develop their abilities, despite MD Charles Levison's genuine enthusiasm for them. They had the worst of both worlds – they were nominally affiliated to a resoundingly unsuccessful independent label, but were in fact under the thumb of a major label uniquely ill-suited to handle them. The more daring and inventive their music, it seemed, the less comfortable Arista felt. John Leckie delivered the finished tapes of *Empires* to the company, then waited for some reaction.

"We didn't hear anything for two weeks. It got to a stage where Jim, Bruce and myself were sending them telegrams. There was Jim sending telegrams from home in Glasgow to Arista, saying 'what a great album stop this album is a hit stop jim kerr glasgow' really just to get some feedback. Then Arista said, 'OK, it's all right, we'll put it out', and that was it. And they'd spent a fortune, they must have spent forty or fifty thousand on that album, recording and everything."

Empires And Dance was released in September 1980. Despite acclaim from the music press, it only reached number 41 in the British album chart, a meagre reward for so forward-looking a record. Insult was added to injury by the fate of the first single taken from it, 'I Travel', released in October. Despite John

Leckie's deluxe all-singing all-dancing 12-inch remix, a treatment to which the song's hurtling mechanized beat was ideally suited, Arista showed little interest or enthusiasm in making the record a hit. Across the Channel, however, it aroused considerably more interest, and at once began to cause a stir in the clubs and discos.

Leckie: "I said to them 'release 'I Travel' as a 12-inch with 'Celebrate' on the other side – it would make a great club mix'. Arista didn't see it but Ariola in France picked it up [the German company, Ariola, distributed Arista's records in Europe, and later bought the label completely]. I think the band went to Paris and said 'hey, listen to this' – they had a cassette of the disco mix I'd done. Ariola immediately snapped up the tape and released it as a 12-inch. It got to about number 12 or 14 in the *Billboard* disco charts. Then there was a demand for it in Britain because I think a few of the music papers had written it up, and Arista had to import five thousand copies off the French. They bought them from France at retail price, so it was costing them money. It was crazy."

CHAPTER 7

The autumn began to look a little brighter when Peter Gabriel, a long-standing hero of the group's, offered the Minds the support slot on his imminent European tour. This was something of a thrill for the band, and indeed the first gig Jim Kerr had ever been to see had been Genesis when Gabriel was still singing with them. He would sometimes cite *The Lamb Lies Down On Broadway* as his favourite LP, and Kerr's own stalking, mysterious stage presence had doubtless been influenced by Gabriel, though in subtle ways. Kerr never went in for the bizarre masks and costumes Gabriel once favoured, but his white-faced, black-eyed appearance and subtly reptilian displays were theatrical enough in their way. Both singers were also aware that stillness could be just as potent a tool as flamboyant, extrovert movement. And behind their stage personae, both were introverted and even shy.

Gabriel had been impressed by *Real To Real Cacophony*, perhaps recognizing a kindred spirit in the album's wayward, frequently uncommercial approach. Despite his status and previous commercial clout, Gabriel himself was beginning to encounter a certain amount of record company hostility to his solo work, perhaps because nobody could tell which of his albums was which since they were all known only as *Peter Gabriel*. But doubts about Gabriel's ponderous progress eventually proved to be unfounded. He pressed on at his own pace until he released *So* in 1986, the album which finally broke him into the multi-million selling bracket. It also featured a guest appearance by Jim Kerr on vocals. Not only was Gabriel rich,

59

with his crafty videos for songs like 'Sledgehammer' and 'Big Time' becoming permanent fixtures on the American MTV network, but he'd kept his integrity and reputation intact.

It was the kind of career pattern which Jim Kerr could envisage forming for Simple Minds, and one which he would welcome. "We've always said that there was something traditional about us," Kerr said. "Like, we admired these bands of the seventies who didn't really come through until their third or fourth album. I think despite trends and fashion we've always come up with something that's been too good to throw away."

Generously, Gabriel also offered to pay the Minds' expenses throughout the tour (he's always taken the trouble to give his support artists a helping hand). The Minds, whose financial situation had become parlous, could hardly believe their luck. The Gabriel tour would introduce them to big European audiences, it would bring them into close proximity with an artist they admired, and perhaps it wouldn't leave them bankrupt. Touring remains a costly operation for all but the biggest artists, the ones who can cover their costs by packing in audiences by the arena-full. For less exalted outfits, playing live is supposed to be its own reward as well as a means of generating record sales, press activity and radio exposure. But financially, touring in itself can involve a band in burdensome debts.

After a show at Hammersmith Palais where they appeared as special guests of Richard Jobson's Skids, the Minds set off for Europe. Another link with their past was broken with the departure of Jane Henderson, whose position as lighting engineer had become increasingly difficult since her brother David quit. Neither David nor Jane felt comfortable in the Rambo-like, all-male world of rock 'n' roll roadcrews, while Jane's relationship with Kerr had made her position in the crew doubly awkward. There was a certain amount of petty muttering among the band that Jane's lighting was designed to flatter Jim while leaving the others in semi-darkness. Then, when her professional competence began to come into question among the rest of the crew, Jane knew the writing was on the wall.

"David didn't have a beer belly and he always felt that

counted against him," she said. "He wasn't macho and he didn't drink pints. Anyway, it was decided I would leave. I knew I was a good lighting engineer, but I wasn't enjoying it any more. Jim had written me a letter, cos they'd had band discussions without him being there – Billy Worton (roadcrew chief) and the rest of the band and Bruce – about how they thought they ought to get a lighting engineer in. Jim wrote to me saying he thought if David hadn't left everything would have been okay, and he was annoyed at the band for sort of selling out, in a way. I think he was quite hurt cos it was like the band were saying they wanted to be like the other bands, kind of thing."

In a sense, they had to be like other bands if they were to compete. They needed the right equipment and a reliable team, but it was inevitable that the whole operation would become less personal as it grew bigger. Outside the tight, creative unit of the five band members, people were as good as the job they did. Much as the band might get to like and trust lighting or sound men, roadies and technicians, all of them were expendable if push came to shove. All that mattered was that Simple Minds got onstage on time every night, and felt comfortable in their work. Offstage, the band could party, go looking for girls or go nightclubbing until dawn, just as long as they were in a fit state by the time the curtain went up the next night. Crews, on the other hand, have to reach the venue well in advance of the band to set up the equipment, then stay long after the show to take it all down again. Then they sometimes end up driving overnight to reach the next gig.

In the event, Jane Henderson didn't much regret abandoning the rock 'n' roll life. "Jim did feel a bit guilty, I think," she mused. "I would come back at maybe five in the morning and I'd been lifting gear and I'd got bruises and things, and, I mean, obviously he can't come offstage and then take down the gear, but I think it was on his conscience, cos his mum and dad would tell him to look after me. And also if the record company took the band out after the gig or something, and there'd be all these girls about, I would feel quite sorry for myself pulling out all these wires and things."

It was a slow process, but despite their problems with Arista, Simple Minds were inching their way upwards onto the international circuit. In this respect, the tour with Gabriel was heaven-sent, introducing them to huge crowds made up of people who were prepared to pay attention to the music, and who weren't just there to take pills, smoke dope and get drunk. The Minds wanted an audience who would make some sort of investment in their music. Despite their credibility with the music press, they weren't interested in remaining a minority-interest cult for the rest of their lives.

Mick MacNeil looked back on that tour fondly a couple of years later. "When we toured Europe with Peter Gabriel, opening gigs to 40,000 people at a time, we were playing to a lot of early Genesis fans, probably aged in their mid-thirties. It was good, because those people are pretty sensible. It's not like they're out to see a punk group or someone like the Clash. They're mature adults and they take music seriously, it's not just a bit of entertainment to them. They stand there and really listen instead of jumping about and screaming. You feel like you've got their complete attention, and that you're doing something for them."

Life on the road with Simple Minds continued to contain more than its fair share of madness and hair-raising moments. One night in Dusseldorf, Derek Forbes displayed amazing presence of mind in saving the life of an apparently deceased German citizen (not long before, Forbes had rescued his then-fiancée, Kay, from drowning when she fell in the river near Rockfield Studios).

"Charlie and I went into town after the gig to get something to eat, and we saw a big crowd of people standing round in a circle. There was this guy lying there, he looked like a drug addict. He was blue. Charlie started freaking, he'd never seen death before and it looked like the guy was dead – he had blood coming out of his nose and his ear, and Charlie was going 'get a fucking ambulance, you German bastards'. I got down beside him and borrowed this guy's glasses and put them up to his mouth and there was breath there, and I punched him in the heart and started giving him a heart massage. My mother was a nurse, so I

62

knew about heart massage, and the next thing, the guy came to. He was completely blue, it was wild, and then he suddenly got up with a start and he was mumbling, and then he walked away! He'd been lying there dead as far as everybody knew, and I just came up and gave it Jesus Forbes."

When they got to Berlin, they ran into John Leckie, who was over there working with an East German band. Leckie knew the owner of a club called Sound Disco in West Berlin, who was keen to get Simple Minds to come down after the Gabriel show. "He said if they'll come down and sign autographs, we'll do a special Simple Minds night and play all Simple Minds records and have a big banquet and vodka. He had rows and rows of these little bottles of Polish and Russian vodka," Leckie explained. "After the show the group walked in, and the place had all these cages with lizards and snakes in. Brian McGee let all the snakes out and everything – they were completely wild, running all over the floor. The place was in an absolute uproar."

Being in Berlin, the group also decided they'd make a trip across the Wall to have a look at the Eastern sector. "We drove around and it was pretty dead," said Leckie. "The group had to be back in the West for a photo session at 4 p.m. When we came through, the soldier at the gate said, can you open the boot? He's speaking in German, and you've got all the Minds talking Scottish, going, 'Och, can't ye speak English?' I had this hired BMW and we couldn't open the boot, and the guard said, 'Wait there,' and went away. We could have been kept there for twelve hours, we were kicking the boot trying to get it open, and everyone's going, 'You okay in there, Fritz?' making out we had someone hidden inside. We saw this little hut with East German soldiers drinking beer. Derek went up to them and said, 'How about a drink?' and just took their beer off them."

Though the touring life is an inexhaustible source of anecdotes after the fact, it's also a major consumer of mental and physical resources. Completely sensible people with children and mortgages begin to twitch and rave after a couple of weeks on the road. U2's guitarist the Edge is a quiet, unassuming character, but even he refers to touring as "The Grand Madness". "Let's face it, it's a very unnatural way to live," he said once.

Touring is exciting and disorientating. Groups are expected to be perpetually sociable and end up sleeping far too little, and probably drinking and smoking too much. Stimulants of one sort or another invariably find their way up the nose, down the throat or into the morning coffee. The whole point of the exercise becomes the urge to keep moving, and, after a few weeks, a tightly-knit bunch of musicians can build up a terrifying head of kinetic energy, looking for new neighbour-hoods to terrorize. Simple Minds generally proved remarkably resilient under the strain, but the pressure was beginning to tell on Brian McGee, the most emotional one of the five. The tension and pace of life may well have provided him with inspiration for his drumming, but he was beginning to wonder vaguely about his sanity and to think seriously about his future with the band.

By the end of 1980, Simple Minds had proved to themselves and to thousands of paying spectators that they were a group with a mission, a force to reckon with. They knew their music was good, and that it was developing all the time. But, at the same time, Arista continued to make appallingly basic errors of judgment, like failing to manufacture enough copes of *Empires And Dance*. The initial pressing was a paltry 7,500 copies, which soon went out of stock. Arista doubled it, but supply was still nowhere near to meeting demand. Then there was the failure of 'I Travel', clearly a potential hit, judging by reaction to it in Europe. For the band, the most frustrating part about 'I Travel' was seeing it in the disco charts and reading about it in the music press, but then discovering that fans couldn't find a copy in the shops.

Relations between Simple Minds and Arista had hit rock bottom. The group now felt so bitter that they issued a press statement apologizing for the non-availability of the 'I Travel' remix, putting the blame squarely on Arista and their "political decision" not to import any more copies. Arista belatedly said they'd import another 5,000, but time was finally up. The Minds' contract with Arista was due for renewal, and the band were determined to leave the label once and for all, whatever it cost.

Returning from their successful European trip, the Minds then set out on a winter British tour which proved to be a dismal let-down. The shows hadn't been promoted properly, and many of the halls they played in were barely half-full. From playing in front of large crowds eager to give their music a chance, the Minds felt that, in their home country, they'd slipped right back to the bottom of the ladder. It was the last straw, particularly for Brian McGee. In November, while Kerr was being interviewed by a raincoat-clad journalist from *Melody Maker* in Sheffield, Bruce Findlay had to dash to the railway station in pursuit of the distraught drummer. McGee had had enough and was on his way back to Glasgow. Findlay just managed to talk him out of it before that night's show.

The situation almost caused an irrevocable rift between the band and Findlay, as Kerr described. "Bruce phoned us up while we were still in Europe on the Gabriel tour. He was going, *'Empires And Dance* went in the chart at 49! And it moved up to 42 this week!' We got back and it was at 68. We thought the tour would be great after the thing with Gabriel, we were treated well and got a good feeling from all of these countries in Europe. But coming back to Britain it really was those worst ones, it was the ones you see on Dr Feelgood's tour sheet, all the Scunthorpes and stuff. We just couldn't fuckin' handle it. There'd be twenty people in a place that could hold 800. Everywhere you looked it was like Ska and Mod, and there just seemed to be no way in for bands even roughly like us, Ultravox or Japan, or something.

"For the first time we knew we'd made a special album and we really felt 'fuck this'. We were playing great songs like 'Constantinople Line' and we were doing all these things onstage, really sort of adventurous, I think. The twenty people who were there thought it was amazing, but it was just crap. Bruce always tries to vibe you up, and in this case he just vibed us up too much. In a sense the picture was sort of distorted, and nobody felt as let down as much as McGee. Bruce came out on two dates and McGee was bubbling and crying and stuff, it was really heavy, and Bruce said, 'Well if I've made you as upset as this, then I'm just going to quit as well.' The catch was we didn't believe he was quitting, we just thought, 'Ah, it's a sinking ship,' which hurt our pride. We cancelled the next five dates or something, and went back to Glasgow. It was great there, because we could still play to a million people and think we were a big band.

"We went through to Bruce in Edinburgh a few days later and said 'you're fucking *out*'. We'd decided at the weekend that we would get ourselves out of Arista, we were a fucking good band and we'd get a new deal. We were gonna get ourselves out or else split up. And we had faith we'd get ourselves out of debt and all these big things. And, as it happens, that's what happened anyway. But I don't know who we thought about getting to manage us. I just don't know what we wanted, to tell the truth. We never saw ourselves as a chart band, but the Human League couldn't get in the charts either, but they could still get 2,000 people to their gigs. And us being a live band, it was much more all these things, like no promotion for the gigs, than frustration at not having a hit single."

Not certain whether they still had a manager or not, the group went to a rehearsal studio in Glasgow to start putting together some new material. After all, if they were going to find a new label, they'd need something to record. Often, Kerr had had conversations with John Leckie about what made a hit single, and whether Simple Minds should consciously set out to write one. The group still clung stubbornly to the notion that writing commercial material was some form of compromise, a betrayal of their artistic pedigree. Leckie thought they'd be better off earning some money, and suggested that Kerr left aside his songs about paranoia and disturbed states of mind and wrote something simple about a boy and girl relationship, a love song. Just for once, just to see what happened.

Kerr went away and thought about this for a while. Leckie was both taken aback and amused when he heard the result of their discussions, which was the deluxe electronic dance track, 'Love Song'. Kerr had taken him at his word while pulling something new out of the band, attaching their growing mastery of pulsating, repeating patterns to the most basic sentiment in pop.

As 'Love Song' was beginning to take shape, a sheepish Bruce Findlay appeared at the studio. He wasn't sure how the meeting with the band would go, or even if they'd let him through the

66

door. The ebullient, bouncing Findlay wasn't used to having his confidence knocked sideways, and the experience had unsettled him considerably. Seeing the group's desperate emotional state on the recent British tour, he'd begun to blame himself for their lack of chart success. He'd even discussed giving up the band's management, but his wife had told him to pull himself together and have a bit more belief in himself. After his divorce a couple of years earlier, he'd married Jane Cowley, the daughter of a wealthy farmer on Scotland's east coast. Jane was evidently strong enough to cope with Bruce's continual absences from home while keeping a critical perspective on her husband's precarious career.

By this time, too, Findlay had acquired a partner in the form of Robert White, previously a lawyer at Arista who'd been involved in negotiating the Simple Minds contract. White was thin, rangy and very English, as great a contrast to Bruce as could have been devised. An expert squash player, he hid a predatory business acumen behind his languid exterior. White had joined Findlay's Schoolhouse Management with a view to participating in the Simple Minds success story, so Bruce wasn't the only one to whom getting the sack was totally unacceptable. White undoubtedly put some pressure on the group to at least reconsider their attitude towards Bruce, and Kerr later admitted his respect for White's toughness. "Robert is the sort of man who'll come into the studio and say, 'I'm only a simple lawyer, I know, but wasn't that violin solo an octave out?'"

Ironically, at the point when the group dropped by to tell Bruce he was fired, he'd re-established his psychological grip on the situation and was feeling chock-full of confidence again. But life's full of surprises.

Findlay's account differs slightly from Kerr's. "They said 'Bruce, since we're making this change with the record company, we've come to this decision that we'd like you to leave as well,'" Bruce reminisced. "I was flabbergasted. I had to believe they'd made the right decision, but as their manager I couldn't let them let me go. They owed me an awful lot of money and I'd have been broke if I'd left, so from a material point of view I was worried. From an ego point of view I was *shattered*. But at the

67

same time I've got such an *enormous* ego that I overcame the impact, I wasn't hurt to the core. I couldn't believe they were being so stupid. I said, 'Look, you're mad, you're wrong.'

"Jim said, 'Look, Bruce, when you said in the van that maybe it was your fault and we should blame you, it was another person talking, that wasn't you and I just lost confidence in you. We need someone with a grand overview, we need someone different. It's because of your lack of confidence.'"

By this point, Findlay's thespian side has almost completely taken over the tale. "I said, 'Well, I'm confident again. I had my moment of doubt. Am I not allowed to expose my moment of weakness? I'm human, for Chrissake, have I got to be superhuman?'"

As Kerr tells it, the band couldn't bear looking at the depressed, deflated figure of their manager-in-limbo standing in the studio, so they all went to the pub across the road. The Minds could be alarming when they fell into a collectively hostile frame of mind, but they eventually relented, grudgingly. "We were wild then," said Kerr. "No matter if we were getting sued to death or put in jail or being hung, drawn and quartered, we'd decided which way it would be. So Bruce was playing with dynamite, I think. He just schmaltzed us into it, he didn't bully us or tactic us because we were just wild."

Fantastically, Arista still hadn't given up all hope of making something out of their troublesome but talented signing. The contract was on the point of expiry, but Arista, in the hope of patching together some sort of solution, threw a lavish party for the band in London. John Leckie was invited, too.

"I had this call from Charles Levison's secretary saying, 'John Leckie, you are invited to a dinner at Morton's in Berkeley Square with Simple Minds.' I said, oh, thank you very much. We all met up in a seedy hotel in Bayswater, and off we went. Arista were trying to convince us, the whole band, to stay with the label, and it was more or less just a big booze-up with fancy food, to say 'aren't we a good record company, chaps?' But it never went beyond that. Jim and Charles Levison had a very heavy discussion which everybody stayed out of, everyone was up there getting into the champagne and there were Jim and

68

Levison really kind of at each other. Jim wouldn't say what was going on.

"Jim's great, he can completely take over the whole thing, he is the man. He can talk to your 14-year-old fan at the stage door or he can talk to the head of Arista Records and just be himself. He doesn't put anything on, he's just himself. He's great. I wish I could be like that."

It was too late for Arista, of course. Kerr told them that the band would split up rather than remain on the label, and he was probably serious. Incredibly, Tarquin Gotch still hadn't got the message. Kerr is convinced that Gotch had fallen hook, line and sinker for the Futurist movement then being lauded in the music press, and that he saw Simple Minds as a potential bandwagon-jumper at a time when other Arista signings – the flyweight Beatles impersonators the Pleasers, the preposterous pseudo-Mods Secret Affair – had abruptly run out of steam. Right on the deadline for the expiry of the Arista contract, Tarquin blithely appeared backstage at The Niteclub in Edinburgh, where the band were playing for three nights to a sympathetic Scottish crowd.

McGee remembers the occasion clearly. "On the second night Tarquin flew up from London and grabbed hold of Jim and tried to get him to get the band together. He was saying 'look, we believe in you, give us a chance' and all this shit. Really wild. They offered us money, the lot. We just said 'sure, fuck off'."

CHAPTER 8

Simple Minds finally parted company with Arista in December 1980, though they wouldn't have been able to if MD Charles Levison hadn't agreed to let them go. Obviously a stubborn, uncooperative Simple Minds would have been of little value to the label, but it hasn't been unknown in the history of the record business for companies to act merely as dogs in the manger, keeping groups under contract to stop anybody else getting them. Whether it was Kerr's apocalyptic threat to destroy the band that did it or just a rational acknowledgment all round that label and group would never get on, Simple Minds were free at last.

In March of the following year, they signed a new deal with Virgin which would bring about an immediate change in their fortunes. Presumably Robert White's intimate acquaintance with the workings of the group's contract with Arista, which he'd helped to draw up, played its part in getting them out of it. Also, the move was eased by the fact that both Arista and Virgin records were distributed in Europe by Ariola, so the headway the group had built up on the Continent was not thrown away. Ariola would still make a percentage on the deal. As it was, Simple Minds had to surrender royalties from their three Arista albums to offset their accumulated debts. But it had to be done.

Polydor also showed interest in the group, perhaps due to the influence of Ian Cranna. By this time, Cranna was working on the pop magazine *Smash Hits* "so I can honestly say that I wasn't angling to be their manager and displace Bruce, although I encouraged the idea of them dispensing with Bruce". He'd contacted people he knew at the record companies, trying to find the group a new home which would prove both profitable and sympathetic.

Virgin finally beat Polydor to the dotted line because of personal interest from both Richard Branson and the label's managing director, Simon Draper. Virgin had, of course, been approached by Bruce Findlay some time earlier, and had kept an eye on the group in the intervening period. Evidently Magazine would never fill Virgin's coffers, but perhaps Simple Minds had qualities which meant they eventually would. They had already demonstrated staying power. Songs as different as 'Chelsea Girl' or 'I Travel' indicated that they had a commercial streak even if they chose to bury it much of the time. Finally, they were incontrovertibly a genuine band, not a singer with backing musicians. The group was all that its members had, so they had to make it work.

For their part, Simple Minds felt that at least part of their trouble with Arista stemmed from the fact that Ben Edmunds, the American A&R man who'd personally pushed through their deal, had left the company soon afterwards, leaving the group with nobody they felt particularly comfortable with at the label's Cavendish Square headquarters. Evidently their contract didn't contain a Main Man clause, which would have allowed for a reassessment of their position in the event of that kind of personnel change within the company. But with the Virgin deal, even if the company were to find itself with a new managing director some day, it seemed reasonable to assume that Richard Branson would be around for some time to come. The Virgin leisure and entertainment empire was his brainchild, even if he sometimes seemed to treat it like a giant game of Monopoly.

Draper and Branson flew up to Glasgow for a trip which combined opening a new Virgin record store in the city with meeting Simple Minds and hearing some new material they'd been working on. The group and Bruce Findlay met the Virgin contingent for lunch at Glasgow's Albany Hotel, and were at once impressed by the streak of madness which Branson hides beneath his outward shyness, a side to his character which would express itself publicly in later years in his exploits in

71

power boats and hot-air balloons. Draper was cooler and more analytical, though he has a reputation in the industry as a man with "good ears" (in other words he knows music when he hears it and can see through trends).

Findlay had asserted flatly to the record company that on no account would the band audition for anybody – their three albums should be proof enough of their capabilities. But the group liked the way negotiations were going, and offered to play Draper and Branson a batch of new songs which they'd pieced together over the last few months. These were 'Love Song', 'The American', 'Sweat In Bullet', 'League Of Nations' and a song called 'Life In Oils' which the group never got around to recording for an album. They'd made demos of the songs back at Glasgow's Ça Va studio, where they'd recorded their very first demo tape, and Mick MacNeil had produced them himself.

By all accounts, the new demos sounded wonderful. John Leckie had come up to Ça Va to do some recording with another local band, Endgames, and the Minds had played him the tapes. "Those first demos of songs that would end up on *Sons And Fascination* were really good," he said. " 'Life In Oils' was great. It was like an oil painting, really kind of misty."

Already, Simple Minds were heading away from the hard, metallic sound of *Empires And Dance* towards a more open-ended, impressionistic kind of funk. The *Empires* songs were stark and strobe-lit, and the dominant colours were black and white. The new material introduced some greys and browns. It was good enough for Virgin, though, characteristically, Branson wanted to chisel away at the demands Findlay put to him on the group's behalf. Nothing, it seemed, amused him more than a spot of boardroom cat-and-mouse, especially when he won. Negotiations therefore continued, since nobody in the Minds camp wanted to put their heads in a noose a second time. There could have been advantages in going to Polydor, too. They'd probably have paid more money, and they also had an American arm which Virgin didn't at the time.

But in the end, the group decided among themselves that Virgin were approaching the deal in the right spirit. Virgin was shrewd enough to realize that Simple Minds had begun to build an audience across Europe even if their progress in Britain had been frustratingly slow. If Virgin could exploit this, it would augur well for a future global base. They were also prepared to cover some of the debts the group had amassed at their previous home, to the tune of some £65,000.

At that point in its history, Virgin was experiencing one of the inevitable downswings that accompany life in a high-risk industry. It had never been renowned as a label which scored masses of spectacular hit singles, and by this time the Sex Pistols had come and gone. Mike Oldfield's early phenomenal success with *Tubular Bells* had left Virgin with the sort of image the company sometimes regretted.

Their former press officer Al Clark, in his Vernon Yard office, described Virgin's predicament at the height of Pistols-mania. "Because Virgin began with *Tubular Bells*, what we'd get would be processions of people in Afghan coats coming up and down the Yard with concept albums complete with artwork ready," Clark said. "What we really wanted, which of course nobody realized at the time because we would have had to have advertised to get it, was a few sort of rowdy records. As far back as 1974, which was when I joined, I remember Simon Draper telling me that he would really like a group like Slade on the label."

Obviously Simple Minds fell some way short of Draper's noisy ideal. But the Virgin catalogue betokened a willingness to sign quality acts and be damned – they had Magazine, XTC, John Lydon's Public Image Ltd and German technopersons DAF, while the Human League were on the point of shedding their dour, experimentalist skin by releasing their mighty electropop album *Dare* onto an ill-prepared world. Still to come was the crashing worldwide success of Culture Club, and in the fullness of time Virgin would also pick up long-distance earners like Phil Collins, Genesis, Peter Gabriel, Bryan Ferry and Steve Winwood. If Virgin made mistakes, it was also a company capable of regenerating itself on the most spectacular scale.

Ian Cranna had observed the negotiations from a distance. "It's a very personal signing. They're signed to Branson and Draper rather than to Virgin. Branson was trying all the old

73

tricks on Jim – 'If you sign to us you have to use Virgin recording studios.' Jim would just sit there and say, 'No, we're not going to'. So Branson and Draper started sweating. Eventually the group got everything they wanted, I think."

Eighteen months after they'd signed with Virgin, Jim reflected on the decision. "When we signed to Arista, they must have told everybody in the building half an hour before we came in, 'There's this woolly band from Scotland somebody's signed, it's a few quid and we've never heard of them but we'd better make them feel all right.' So you got taken round every department, everybody said 'great to meet you', everybody had half an hour to talk to you and give you a cup of tea and bluff that they knew a bit about you. On the day I thought it was great – 'The whole company likes us! Couldn't get a better label, Lou Reed's on it and Iggy Pop and Patti Smith. It'll be brilliant!' And of course two months later you realize how stupid the whole thing is.

"When we signed with Virgin, we knew that some people in the building were into us but others had reservations, because Magazine and XTC and the Human League weren't doing well. We looked in the different departments and everyone just went 'oh' and they really were just too fucking busy, it wasn't just bullshit. On the day we thought, 'Huh, some welcome.' It was the best way to start, we knew we had to impress everybody in there. Now we feel we're one of their best-liked bands, not in terms of money, just in terms of people and respect, because we work and we get things done and if we argue, it's good."

Changes were in the air from the start. Within a week of signing their new contract, the Minds were introduced to Steve Hillage as their potential new producer, apparently at Simon Draper's suggestion. On the face of it, the idea was absurd. If anybody had an opinion about Hillage at all, it was that he was a spaced-out hippy guitar player in a woolly hat, half-man, half-vegetable.

His recording career had begun in 1969 with an album called *Arzachal* on a label called Uriel, so even then his mystical tendencies were well developed. At Kent University around 1970, Hillage became involved with a pool of musicians who fell in and out of groups like Caravan, Hatfield and the North,

Henry Cow and Gong, mixing a loosely jazz-based experimentalism with more rock-derived ideas. Then Hillage moved into session work and met Kevin Ayers, on whose *Bananamour* album his playing may be heard. Hillage was touring with Ayers in France when his path crossed with Gong's once again, and, overcome with nostalgia, he joined them instead. He made three albums with the group (possibly four, but sleeve notes and memories are unreliable), then veered off into solo work with albums like *L.*, *Motivation Radio*, and *Green*, all for Virgin.

However, perhaps Draper wasn't so wide of the mark after all, since although Hillage was still known to be fond of holding conversations with plants and rarely left home without first scouring his horoscope for propitious astrological activity, the latter two albums had found him pursuing a direction which could only be labelled "funk". Perhaps the shrewd Virgin MD perceived possible new bearings for Simple Minds before anybody else did. Coincidentally, too, Hillage had known Bruce Findlay since the Gong days. Bruce's Records had brought the group over from France for their first British tour around the time of their *Camembert Electrique* album, although Hillage didn't join the band until later.

Virgin evidently had faith in Hillage as a producer, and had already been putting him into the studio to produce new artists like Ken Lockie and Ross Middleton's Positive Noise. Kerr and Burchill heard some of the Lockie material and were immediately impressed. "It was this really incredible sound," Burchill enthused, "it was really open and sparse, it was a big heavy drum thing and the sax was incredible."

That settled it. They'd also been thinking in terms of using either Martin Rushent or Steve Lillywhite, but Rushent wasn't available and they decided Lillywhite was too expensive, though they would work with him subsequently. Simple Minds had a brief tour of clubs on the American East Coast to fulfil, and decided that after that they'd begin recording with Hillage. Hillage himself commented: "The group didn't want to make an obvious assembly-line choice of producer. I think Simple Minds have always wanted to achieve success without necessarily going down the conventional route."

By this time, the band had been joined on the road by Kerr's younger brother Paul. He'd given up a possible future as a footballer with the Glasgow club Celtic, with whom he'd had several promising trial games, and worked his passage onto the road crew. Football's infighting and bitter power-politics had eventually proved too much for him to cope with. Like rock music, football was a glamorous and elusive escape route from the confines of working-class life.

Jim and Charlie could remember taking Paul to see Mott the Hoople and Steve Harley at the Glasgow Apollo when he was twelve. Later, when Johnny and the Self Abusers were playing at the Doune Castle pub, Paul (still too young to drink) had been smuggled inside hidden in the case for Brian McGee's bass drum. But being Jim's brother didn't mean automatic preferential treatment. Quite the opposite, in fact, since while Burchill and Forbes were impressed by how Paul had learned to maintain and set up their stage equipment and instruments, Jim was dubious about giving him a full-time job since he thought it might look like nepotism. Honour demanded that Paul had to meet the most stringent requirements. "My mum and dad said get him a job if you can," Jim remembered. "I said I can't, he's got to do it off his own bat."

The band completed their American dates a little earlier than they anticipated, since Brian McGee's allergy to touring surfaced once again and this time he couldn't be prevented from returning home before the group had played their scheduled final gig. The others were not amused, but followed him back to London and went straight into Farmyard Studios in Amersham, where they'd recorded *Life In A Day*, to begin working on 'The American'. It was understood that McGee's position with the group would be under review during the subsequent period of recording.

From any rational viewpoint, it was becoming obvious that McGee's days with the band were numbered. After the American shows, he was overcome with nervous exhaustion, and spent ten days in bed, in tears much of the time. "I should have been stronger and fought that sickness," he said, looking back. "But I didn't, I just collapsed." He reckoned that he wouldn't have been able to pull through without the support of his wife-to-be, Shirley.

For the immediate present, all energies were focused on making the next album. Nobody bothered to mention to John Leckie that his services would no longer be required, but he took it in good part. "Well, they don't tell you, do they?" he chortled ruefully. "You read it in the *Melody Maker*. But it was great for them that they were in the studio with someone else, because they'd only ever been in the studio with me. Steve Hillage was OK, I guess he was quite a musical producer. Maybe they learned more about the songs and the melodies and things, cos what they were really lacking on *Empires And Dance* and *Real To Real* were the actual melodies."

Leckie harbours only positive emotions about Simple Minds, particularly Kerr's pivotal role in the band. "I really respect him and I love him, actually. A lot of his interviews have nothing to do with music, they're all about spirit – it's really drumming everyone up and getting everyone's spirits up and saying let's get out there and do it, let's stop sitting around being dull, let's be alive. It's great that he can do that, and that's the whole spirit of Simple Minds and he really is the leader."

Steve Hillage was also overwhelmed by the experience of working with the determined bunch of Scotsmen. "Among all the dross of present day pop music, I think there are a few bands that stick out and convey a rich sense of spirit in their music," he noted afterwards. "Simple Minds are one of them, and I would say U2 and Echo and the Bunnymen also are in that category, and I like them very much as well.

"But I still find Simple Minds the most interesting, partly because they're not just a guitar band. They've also got the synthesizers, and I think Mick MacNeil is a really brilliant keyboard player. He's very original as well, he's got a kind of Eno element and a jazz-rock element and also a sort of Highland element, and they're all mixed up. Mick and Charlie together are a very formidable team. And they've also got a funk-dance element, particularly the bass, so I find their music the most wide-ranging of those three groups.

"People are always trying to put groups into various brackets, and with *Life In A Day* I think they were looked at as a kind of nouveau-pop band à la Japan, then they were the bleak industrial band, then there was this kind of New Genesis thing which I thought was a bit ridiculous – but they're Simple Minds. Now other bands are referred to as 'a bit like Simple Minds'. They've basically developed their own category. I was particularly interested to work with them because I could relate to a lot of the underlying spirit of their music."

The group and their new producer initially worked fast, and 'The American' was released as a single in May 1981. The song had been written as a result of the group's visits to the States, and while the sound of the track once more suggested motion and travel, the claustrophobic Europaranoia of *Empires And Dance* had been replaced with imagery of search and quest. America, the big country, allowed the eye and the mind to travel further and wider. "What do you know about this world, anyway?" Kerr wanted to know, suggesting that he was damn well going to find out.

The song didn't make much of a dent on the charts, but would enjoy a long and fruitful life in discos and clubs, where its juddering beat and sense of adventure set it apart from the frozen totalitarian sound of Spandau Ballet or the quasi-orchestral kitsch of Ultravox's 'Vienna'. A 12-inch version was also released for clubland purposes, though (mysteriously) it seemed to be identical to the 7-inch.

As Kerr would point out, echoing Steve Hillage, the press were, as usual, uncertain whether to lump Simple Minds in with the so-called New Romantics or to slide them in alongside U2 and the Bunnymen. "We must confuse a lot of people. We're the only band I know that can get compared on one hand to Heaven 17, Kraftwerk, the Human League and a few more, yet at the same time get compared to the Comsat Angels, Joy Division and the Bunnymen. The great thing about us is that the spirit's so big that it could never be broken by anything like that."

The Minds obstinately continued to defy categorization, and if that meant they were denied the supernova chart action of the Durans and Spandaus, it also meant they never became so hip that a fall from grace was inevitable.

CHAPTER 9

'Love Song' was released as a second single in July 1980, a trailer for the *Sons And Fascination/Sister Feelings Call* double LP set two months later. Again, there was a thrilling sense of purpose in the Minds' new music, and Kerr would explain later that the song was supposed to embody a sense of optimism which flew in the face of the unemployment and negativity the group had encountered back in Glasgow. "I love success," he said. "I love to see winners." 'Love Song' was built on one of their great rolling riffs, and MacNeil's robotic synth introduction perhaps glanced back to Hillage's European experiences with Holger Czukay and Cologne-based producer Conny Plank. Surely music like this couldn't be kept in the wings for much longer.

Completion of the new album was, however, complicated by both the nature of the personalities involved and by the especially fertile state of mind the group found themselves in. Hillage managed to unearth some cut-price studios, like Park Gates in Sussex, in which the group could afford to jam and experiment together without spending a fortune, but it turned out to be a false economy. In retrospect, they should have planned the sessions more thoroughly and then recorded in a good studio. Every day they went into the studio, the Minds would breed a new sound or a new idea which seemed too good not to follow up. A profusion of half-finished backing tracks began to be amassed on tape. Nobody knew where it would end, and Hillage didn't seem to want to tell them to stop, although he insists he tried to put his foot down in the end.

"Actually we had a little bit of a problem about this. Basically the group had come up with about fourteen or fifteen ideas, all of which were good. I was quite adamant that it should be fined down to about eight or nine to make a single album. Eventually the group just couldn't bring themselves to do it, for them it was like tragedy and they wanted to do all the tracks. So the idea of doing two albums was eventually adopted."

Charlie Burchill is more scathing. "Even halfway through, that album never really had any proper direction. We were still writing as if we had unlimited time. We couldn't figure out how we were gonna complete all these tracks, we couldn't separate which ones we were gonna go with, so we decided to do the lot. That's when Hillage started losing the place. A producer's being paid to have discipline and be objective. He should have stopped all that earlier on.

"Also it was only about the second thing he'd ever produced, so it was a bit rash of us to go in on the strength of that Ken Lockie thing. He hadn't been doing it long enough to develop his own technique in the studio. He was doing these all-night sessions and he listens to things incredibly loud, and his ears were just fucking knackered, you know."

The record company became concerned, and Hillage began to receive big-brotherish phone calls from Simon Draper. That he was a musician himself perhaps explained Hillage's reluctance to curb the group's frantic creativity – he was more naturally sympathetic to the group's inclinations than to Virgin's strictures on time and budget. But pressure was mounting on him from all sides, and he made a bad error in the band's eyes by blaming them for writing too many songs instead of getting down to finishing the job. He was supposed to be on their side, after all.

"I came in and Jim said to me, 'He's just blamed us for this, that and the next thing on the album,' in front of him," Burchill recounts. "I was really wild, and I was going to him, 'You fucking grassed the band to the record company!' It was just like kids. Then, after that, Hillage was doing a mix and he went, 'Palpitations, palpitations!' and he fell off his seat, ran away to his car and just bombed off to hospital. So us and the engineer had to do the mix. In fact the engineer wasn't even there, but the mix was half set up and we just completed it. We were *that much* from phoning John Leckie to get him to salvage the album. Fucking ridiculous."

Still, the results were eventually a good deal more impressive than some of the recording traumas might have suggested. "It gave us a lot of heartache but it wasn't really as bad as that, it wasn't a really tormenting period," Burchill added. "Maybe eighty per cent of it was really good fun and really rewarding. We came out with what I think's a really classic achievement for the amount we took on in that period."

The engineer for the Farmyard Studios sessions was Hugh Jones, now a producer in his own right. He remembers *Sons And Fascination* as being a slightly stressful period in his life.

"The group really liked Steve Hillage," he said. "You can't dislike Hillage, it's impossible, he's a lovely, lovely chap. I think he should maybe have come down on the group harder. The group wanted to spend as much time as they could, fair enough, but you had to temper that with realities. When Simple Minds got in the studio, they lost all sense of perspective – they couldn't see the wood for the trees."

Despite their new relationship with Virgin, there was still some sense of frustration that Simple Minds hadn't yet achieved the kind of status they felt their records and their years of effort entitled them to. They were artistically mature, but not commercially.

"The group were in a funny frame of mind at that point," said Jones. "They wanted to do what they wanted to do, that hadn't changed, but their desire for a commercial success was starting to show itself. I remember one breakfast or lunchtime when 'The American' went down in the charts and they were really, *really* pissed off. They really wanted a hit. This was their fourth album and they wanted to spend the time that a fourth album warrants, but without commercial success behind them they didn't have the financial clout to do it."

Add to all this the fact that Brian McGee was finally in the process of leaving the band, and it's some wonder that the albums were ever finished at all. With the sessions finally complete, Hillage took the tapes to Regent's Park studios in London for mixing and overdubs. By now, with time running over and money running out, pressure from Virgin was becoming intense. Hugh Jones: "By that time the big guns from Virgin were coming out a little bit. Simon Draper and Steve Lewis would come down, and they'd play classic policemen – it was brilliant, Mr Nice and Mr Nasty. Simon was saying, 'Well, of *course* you can carry on doing this, it'll be all right.' Then Lewis would come in with, 'But if you do, you can forget the tour.'"

The strain began to tell on the harrassed Hillage. "I came very close to cracking myself up physically, actually," he admitted. "If it wasn't for the fact that it was very invigorating and inspiring music I don't think I would have been able to work so hard."

Hillage might have picked an easier band to work with, as Mick MacNeil pointed out. "I think the humour in the band's quite wild – people who aren't really familiar with it get offended by it. But it wasn't really that that freaked Hillage out, it was the amount of work we had to get done. He never expected that. It freaked us out a wee bit as well. We got all the material we wanted done, which was really good, but it was like putting off making decisions until the last minute, how long tracks should be and generally not being too prepared. From now on I think we should know exactly which songs we're doing and how long they'll last on each side of the album."

From the group's point of view, their producer was growing increasingly eccentric before their eyes. "He fell off his chair one night," Burchill remembered. "There were these three steps he had to go up to the mixing desk, and he was sitting in this swivel chair and he always used to scratch his balls and pick his nose while he was mixing. It was total concentration and you couldn't break it. He used to rock and get into a trance, then one night he was swivelling about in his chair and he was getting into it, and then he suddenly went, 'Aaargh!' and fell off his chair and down the steps. He was lying there going, 'Oh bastard! Fucking stairs!' and all that, halfway through the mix. And he had to start again. Fucking classic."

Even when they'd left the studio for the night, there was no respite from the weird behaviour being brought on by the sessions. "Hillage used to do these all-night sessions, then in the morning he'd be driving us back," said Charlie. "He hated the police, he used to call them 'the swine' and 'pigs', and he'd drive up to traffic lights at eight in the morning after an all-nighter. There'd be a traffic policeman on a bike and Hillage would open the window, say, 'Go home, you cunt,' and then roll the window up again."

Hillage brought out something quite new in Simple Minds' music. Some of the *Sister Feelings Call* half of the double set sounded half-finished and scrappy, presumably because it was. 'Careful In Career', for instance, contains a couple of interesting ideas and noises which aren't developed, while 'League Of Nations' is basically a beat with a bit of vocal on top. 'Sound In 70 Cities' is simply an instrumental remix of '70 Cities As Love Brings The Fall', from *Sons And Fascination*, and has been tacked on as a makeshift coda.

On the other hand, *Sister Feelings* also contained 'The American', as well as 'Theme For Great Cities', a speedy instrumental which must have been designed as an in-car accessory for long journeys. If Kraftwerk had ever allowed themselves to drink a little too much schnapps and kick their shoes off, perhaps they could have sounded like this. Still, Mick MacNeil reckoned 'Theme' could have been better still if they'd had more time and thought things through more thoroughly.

"It was a problem, because we only found out which tracks would be instrumental towards the end of the album," said Mick. "I never imagined 'Theme For Great Cities' being an instrumental while Jim would say that he *always* imagined it being an instrumental. But had I known that it was going to be and borne that in mind, I'm sure it would have been much more interesting, even though I think it's a classic."

But it was on *Sons And Fascination* that the real signs of growth could be discerned, and the disc displayed a new awareness of tone and texture as well as an overall sense of unity. *Sons* opens with 'In Trance As Mission', a seven-minute scene-setter. Forbes and McGee hit a resolute stride as Burchill floats high, droning lines above MacNeil's watercolour keyboards. Kerr's

83

vocal found him in a visionary frame of mind – "for just one moment in time I hear the holy backbeat" – and the song suggests both enormous distance and a faintly mystical sense of expectation.

The dreamlike feeling of quest hinted at any number of literary models, though Kerr put it all down to the hours he'd spent in the band's bus rolling down America's blue highways. "I wanted to take the repetition and loneliness of a highway, and because you're travelling you've got no roots, no bearings – you just keep going and all you've got is your own thoughts."

Originally, Hillage had had doubts about opening the collection with 'In Trance', but after he'd lived with it for a while he agreed with the band's decision. "I thought the song was a bit long, but in retrospect it's so emphatically strong in putting over the overall vibe of the whole record, it's a really good first track. Charlie had this one note that goes right the way through, because he can sustain his guitar with the feedback, and then he had some harmonics and we faded them in at various spots."

Indeed, the interplay between Burchill and Hillage, both guitar players, perhaps resolved some doubts in Charlie's own mind about his role in the still-developing Simple Minds set-up. "On *Empires And Dance* there were wee bits here and there that I regret a bit," said Charlie. "There were a couple of things I did that were too close to the keyboards – people couldn't hear it, they couldn't tell what was doing what. With *Sons* I think we did better, because there we managed to use the technology with basic sounds. The more expensive Mick's instruments get and the more technology he introduces, the simpler the pieces get and the simpler the sounds become."

John Leckie noticed the change, too. "On the first album Charlie was writing the songs and he was very much the dominant musician in the whole thing. Then I think he got a bit confused during *Real To Real* and *Empires*; I don't think he quite knew what place the guitar was going to take in the music because it was so synth and bass-drum orientated. With *Sons And Fascination* he found a really sort of unique style. He had an effects board with every gadget imaginable with his guitar going through all of them, and he was playing actually quite minimally."

Whereas in earlier days the Minds might have been overawed by the reputation of somebody like Steve Hillage, by now they were imperturbably confident in their own skills. "Hillage was a brilliant musician and I respected him as such," said Kerr. "Then one night him and Charlie plugged into the same amplifier, and even Hillage would admit Charlie ran absolute riot with him. The reason I find it so hard to accept is that I knew Charlie when he couldn't play a single chord."

Hillage has no hesitation in singing Burchill's praises. "He's a really original guitar player. As a guitarist I really enjoyed working with Charlie, and I learned quite a lot from his approach, actually. Some of the lines he picks out in songs are very far from what the average guitarist would pick out. Sometimes you don't even know it's a guitar."

"I was talking to Steve Hillage about Robert Fripp," Burchill remembered, "and I was saying I thought that quite a lot of guitar was just pure maths. There's certain things you realize are just like sums or puzzles, and once you find the solution to them it opens up so many doors. We did a song called 'Twentieth Century Promised Land' and we stumbled across these chords. It wasn't just the chords that made the whole thing, it was a combination of the chords, what the bass was doing and what I was doing. As soon as we hit it everybody went, 'Right, that's it,' and we had to work in reverse and figure out what we'd done – we didn't have a clue what had happened."

After 'In Trance As Mission', the first side of *Sons And Fascination* became angular and more funk-based. 'Sweat In Bullet' and '70 Cities' both tended to make more sense onstage, where they were fuller and more tactile, though Pete Walsh later devised a 12-inch remix of 'Sweat' which kicked a good deal harder than the album verson. In both tracks, Burchill and MacNeil produced an intricate counterpoint of sounds and rhythms which snapped together around Forbes' drilling bass-lines. Perhaps this is what Hillage meant when he said the collection "has a sort of edge and ferocity which I hadn't felt on the previous albums – it kicks arse". Then in 'Boys From Brazil', McGee had a chance to shine with a pummelling backbeat which set off Kerr's lyric about brutalized innocence and guilt warped into decadence – "babies cannot handle crocodiles". The title had been borrowed from Ira Levin's book about Führer-clones in South America, though Kerr had had British neo-Nazis like the National Front in his sights when he wrote it.

The second side of *Sons* was really the heart of the matter. After the rolling thunder of 'Love Song', the rest of the disc was taken up with a trio of songs which form a kind of suite, and share the same haunted instrumental tints. 'This Earth That You Walk Upon' seemed to be an eerie deliberation on mortality, full of shadowy keyboards and banshee guitar. 'Sons And Fascination' is a glide through misty Highland glens on some forgotten dawn, MacNeil's bagpipe synths and a slow-marching drum machine suggesting the ghosts of Culloden. There was no mistaking the distinctively Scottish timbre of these songs, MacNeil in particular dealing in tones which suggested mountain air and the tang of heather. Just for a while, perhaps he was back on Barra.

The concluding 'Seeing Out The Angel' was the perfect endgame for the LP, a logical extension of the preceding tracks but also a dimension removed from them. It's an exquisite distillation of stillness, awe measured in fine calibrations. It has the unmistakable feel of a requiem, stemming not only from Kerr's rapt vocal but from MacNeil's churchy chords and Burchill's church-bell guitar chimes. The Catholic heritage of terror and wonder had its uses, after all.

"There's one line from 'In Trance As Mission' that always freaks me out when I hear it," said Kerr. "'I hear the holy backbeat.' Y'know, it's like a Godly sort of Catholic thing. Those songs – 'Seeing Out The Angel', 'This Earth That You Walk Upon', 'In Trance' – I don't know if it's a sort of godly feeling, or something. No one in the group practises religion, but most of the band are Catholic. I think you get stamped with that when you're young and it's there forever, you can't really escape it."

This was the sort of music that could work mysterious changes in the receptive listener, anyone who didn't just dismiss it as synthesizer art-rock. "They were coming out of a period of being associated with bleak industrial music," said Hillage, "and they were entering a period where they were exploring much more colourful music. I sort of wanted to help them make that transformation. I mean, things like 'Seeing Out The Angel' – you wouldn't really imagine that being on *Empires And Dance*. It's got a new colour. 'Angel' is amazing, I adore that track."

Hillage also estimates that although the lack of military-style studio discipline caused everybody all kinds of grief in trying to finish two albums in the time allotted for one, it did allow for some of the album's strongest pieces to be written. Many of the best songs might have gone missing had deadlines been slammed down on the band earlier on.

"In fact, 'Seeing Out The Angel' was one of the last tracks to really form itself, and 'This Earth That You Walk Upon' as well, which is another track I really like. That one came out of a jam. We were mixing 'Love Song' to be released as a single and Mick was jamming in the studio with a drum machine, echo box and his keyboards. We suddenly noticed there was this amazing sound coming out, so we grabbed a bit of it on the two-track recorder as a demo. Then we took the drum machine and made it into a tape loop. Then we built the song on top of that, and if we'd just been going for a single album we'd have lost that one as well. So it was swings and roundabouts."

There seemed to be an air of predestination about some of the music, as though it was meant to be written and recorded in spite of anybody's efforts to rein it in. Whether the world at large would buy it or not was anybody's guess, but the group pressed on regardless. "We did 'This Earth'," said Burchill, "and there was this bit in the middle where I played this sort of solo. Total accident, I was just jamming it in the studio. Jim was sitting there and he went, 'fucking beautiful, by the way, that's brilliant,' then Mick heard it and Mick said the same. I listened to it back and I thought, great and thought maybe that was the end of it, that was the acclaim for that idea. After that, maybe 10,000 people say they love it, but it doesn't really strike you because it's already been established that it was good and it was liked."

Steve Hillage's working partnership with the band didn't continue and it had obviously been fraught with assorted difficulties, but something valuable had come from it. "This might sound a bit silly," Hillage mused, "but there's so much of the sort of underlying spirit of their music which corresponds to some of the things that I was into in my music, although I expressed it in vastly different ways because obviously I'm a different person from a different background, that I feel to a certain extent there was a slight element of destiny in working with them. When we met we had a rapport, and I got things out of it and I'm sure they got things out of it."

CHAPTER 10

With the album finished, and with Simple Minds at a point where they felt at last that the sort of success they deserved was at least dimly visible on the horizon, Brian McGee finally handed in his notice. McGee was not only a founder-member of the band and an old friend of Kerr and Burchill from schooldays, but he'd also become a central figure in the group's mythology; the star of numerous anecdotes. Although the writing had been on the wall for a year or more, the emotional impact of his departure still came as a severe blow to all of them.

McGee had decided he wanted to marry the girlfriend he'd been with for several years, Shirley McLean, and couldn't face the prospect of endless touring and staying in anonymous hotels. He needed a home life. Probably, had he made a firm declaration of intent to the band and taken a kind of oath of renewed allegiance, they'd have overlooked his panicky return from their last American shows and welcomed him back into the fold. But McGee felt he was emotionally too far gone for that at the time.

He described the pressures which had finally persuaded him he had to go. "I don't know how any of the band got through the *Sons And Fascination* album, because halfway through I was making decisions about whether I was leaving or not. And we were still trying to concentrate on the music. It was really, really fucked up and tense. Steve Hillage was no good for me at that stage, because what I needed was someone stable to keep things organized. He overworked us, took us too far beyond our means. That album should have been cut down to a single record.

"It was a thousand and one things, really. My health – I was really sick at the time. I was seven stone and I was eating like a pig, but for some reason it had no effect. I was sick of touring, I really wasn't keen on it. Well, I liked touring, but the way the band tours, you just don't live anywhere. You drift. It's just like a crusade, carry on anywhere as long as it's somewhere new. I quite like the comforts of home at times, y'know, to keep me secure and keep me sane, but it wasn't happening that often towards the end.

"Before I left we discussed it. We knew something was going to happen, whether it would be a long-term thing or whatever. The band were going to carry on. I said to them before I left, 'I know next year it's going to be big,' and that's probably one of the reasons I wanted to leave as well, because I didn't want to be involved *then* and then decide to leave. It was getting bigger, more successful, more demanding, and if I left then it would have been really horrible for them, and for me, to start breaking up at that point. When I left the band I didn't lose any faith, I just had to get out for my own personal reasons."

McGee's departure posed problems on a musical level, too. His drumming was never flashy or full of exotic technique, but everyone who's worked with him has been impressed with his time-keeping and uncomplicated power. He was also a more than capable back-up singer. "Fantastic time-keeping," enthused Steve Hillage. "On nearly all the tracks we did the tempo is absolutely unswerving, and yet we didn't use a click-track (a kind of metronome), apart from, I think, on 'The American'. Brian had also developed a way of getting a non-snare sound from a snare drum, which I liked. So with him leaving, the group lost a certain element."

John Leckie rated McGee highly as a musician too, but wasn't surprised when he heard he'd left the band. "I think the big thing was the pressure of touring and being away from home," said Leckie. "He hated being in America. I think he probably hated being in Europe, actually. I don't think he really liked committing himself totally, and in the Minds you have to."

Considering the band's insane touring schedule and reckless disregard for such staples as sleep or food, it was only surprising

Johnny and the Self Abusers in 1977, at Glasgow Zhivagos (*above*) and the Crown Hotel, Wishaw. 'It was a great period, it shaped a lot of the attitudes we've got now,' said Charlie Burchill (*Peter McArthur*)

Mick MacNeil, the synth player from Barra, models the dark, silent look favoured by Simple Minds in their early days (*Richard Coward*)

Charlie Burchill and Jim Kerr, friends since pre-school days, formed the original core of Simple Minds (*S. Glyn-Jones*)

The Notorious Kerr Brothers, Paul (*right*) and Jim. Paul is now Simple Minds' tour manager (*Adam Sweeting*)

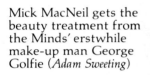

Mick MacNeil gets the beauty treatment from the Minds' erstwhile make-up man George Golfie (*Adam Sweeting*)

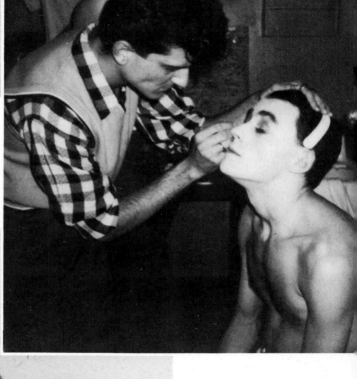

Derek Forbes with his parents, Elizabeth and Henry (*Derek Forbes*)

Minds' manager Bruce Findlay greets his public as then-drummer Kenny Hyslop prepares to lower away (late-'81) (*Derek Forbes*)

Former tour manager and guru Lenny Love, a familiar face from the Edinburgh circuit (*Derek Forbes*)

Jim Kerr, Glasgow, 1982
(*Adam Sweeting*)

Mel Gaynor, slapper of necks
(*Adam Sweeting*)

Mick and Charlie consider the state of London Transport (*Derek Forbes*)

Local hero Jim Kerr gives a fan a leg-up, at a personal appearance to launch the live album *In The City of Light* (*Syndication International*)

Celtic soul brothers Kerr and Bono, somewhere in Europe, 1983 (*Richard Bellia*)

Hymn to her – Jim and Chrissie Hynde in moment of connubial bliss
(*Robert Mathew/Retna*)

that McGee was the sole casualty. Each of the others had a way of dealing with the strain, and even of thriving on it. Mick MacNeil was capable of withdrawing into himself to think about music in the abstract, his theoretical training leaving him well equipped to deal with musical problems as mathematical puzzles in his head. Geography didn't seem to worry him. "Sometimes you can be doing a really long tour and you're stuck in Norwich or somewhere," he said. "That's when the tour's rotten. But the first night in New York and you're away. That's basically what the whole thing's for. Just go out and play."

Charlie Burchill has a frenetic streak which allows him to read two or three novels simultaneously, listen to a range of music which might span Bach, Little Feat and anything in between, and sleep for only two or three hours a night. As for Forbes, his robust personality and unquestioning self-confidence allowed him to stroll through the most nightmarish scenes without batting an eyelid, although he has been known to throw a punch at trouble-makers from time to time. You could often catch him drawing cartoons in a sketchpad for relaxation, usually concerning the obscene adventures of Dan Yer Man (a thinly-disguised version of himself).

Kerr, too, could switch off from outside distractions, to consider the band's next career move, muse over their long-term strategy or just ponder changes in the running order for their live shows. He'd often withdraw to his hotel room or the back of the tour bus to give himself time and space to think, and it was implicitly understood that he wanted to be left alone. Even when he was in a room full of people, you'd suddenly become aware that he had simply ceased to be involved in the crosstalk and conviviality around him.

It came naturally to him to keep his thoughts to himself, and he habitually presented an inscrutable façade to outsiders or, when necessary, to close acquaintances. "Trying to find emotions in that man or telling what he's thinking is hard," Brian McGee observed. Decisions would quietly be taken, perhaps after a discussion between Jim and Bruce Findlay either in person or over the telephone, and would be silently implemented as though by mysterious telepathic intervention. The

91

group would adopt the chosen policy, perhaps about the where and when of recording or touring, and would talk about it thereafter as if everybody had known this was what would happen all along. It resembled a form of government by willpower.

Everybody appeared content with this state of affairs except Brian McGee. For him, life on the road seemed to be more of a permanent condition of conflict, both with the other Minds and within himself. "Brian was a very passionate drummer and put a lot into his drumming physically, which subsequent replacements didn't do," was how Ian Cranna saw it. "He was also a very good singer and backing vocalist. But one of the reasons I'm sure he was so passionate was that he and the band didn't always see eye to eye. There'd be arguments and Brian would take it out on his drums, I think."

"I don't think I'm the greatest drummer in the world," Brian said, "but for what I was doing with the band I was adequate. It was a contribution that was not all technical, but more heart."

The emotional factor would be the hard part of McGee's contribution to replace. Typically, the group stayed close to home when they went looking for a new drummer. Throughout their career they've maintained a Scottish core at the centre of the operation, however big it's become. Roadcrew members have been recruited from the Glasgow and Edinburgh circuit wherever possible, and the band have continued to work with local Scottish promoters Pete Irvine and Barry Wright, alias Regular Music, who have been booking Simple Minds' shows in Scotland from the band's earliest days.

They soon decided on Kenny Hyslop as the new man behind the kit. Hyslop had played with the Zones, one of the bands who'd recorded on the Zoom label, and if he was never destined to fit into the group's complicated jigsaw of personalities, at least he was a familiar Scottish face. He was also a forceful drummer who could contribute his own musical ideas. The Minds hired Hyslop for a trial period and waited to see how it worked out. The band had spent years painstakingly building their particular internal rapport, and were in no hurry to wreck the delicate balance by hastily hiring the wrong man. "We like him a lot but he's got his fingers in lots of different pies," Kerr explained. "I don't think we will try and get a permanent drummer."

McGee's absence did nothing to lessen the group's ambition and growing sense that they were beginning to achieve their objectives. Perhaps there was even a sense of relief that the drummer's long-threatened departure had finally come. Encouragingly, there was now evidence to reinforce the group's optimism. *Sons And Fascination/Sister Feelings Call* was released as a special-edition double-pack in September 1981 (the two records were split and sold separately later on). The collection entered the British album chart at number 14, and peaked at 11, far and away the Minds' best chart performance up to that time.

Their touring schedule remained packed, and now took them farther afield than ever. With the new album just released, the band said a temporary goodbye to the UK with a show at the Hammersmith Odeon in September, a concert which also resulted in a permanent farewell to sound engineer Billy Worton. The band's sound that night was, by all accounts, atrocious, a report borne out by the catastrophically fuddled live recording of 'In Trance As Mission' which later turned up on the B-side of Pete Walsh's remix of 'Sweat In Bullet', released that November. Worton was fired on the spot.

The group then headed west for some more American dates, recruiting a new sound engineer, Frank Gallagher, en route. Gallagher was a transplanted Glaswegian living in New York, and both worked and played at a frenetic pace which Simple Minds could appreciate. They played a few shows in Canada too, which sowed the seeds for steady sales of *Sons And Fascination* in the ensuing weeks. Then they flew on to Australia to play their first-ever concerts there, and immediately struck up a strong rapport with their audiences. There was clearly a home for Simple Minds in the countries of the old Commonwealth, whatever might happen elsewhere.

Virgin had its own operation in Australia, and the company had already set up successful visits Down Under by Magazine and XTC. The existence of a fully-functioning Australian arm of the record label helped push the new album into the local charts for a lengthy stay and sales of 40,000 copies, not many by

American or even British standards but exceedingly healthy for the Antipodes. 'Love Song' also made the Top 10 in the Australian singles chart.

Australia, with its vast and empty landscapes, made a big impression on the band. This was what Icehouse, the Australian group with whom Simple Minds toured before playing their own shows, had dubbed the Great Southern Land. The punishing distances and parched open spaces left their mark on Kerr, in particular. "In Australia we did some long drives," he said. "We drove from Brisbane to Sydney and I found that staring out of the window induced a trance-like state. I was looking at the sky and it was like seeing the sky for the first time. We drove through what looked like petrified forests or like forests which were silver-white and looked dead. Maybe I was drunk or something, but I just felt things, spiritual things. For the first time I began to think about the world as an old place. I just started to think about things and then I wrote them down. That's the way I've been working for two years." The group's travel correspondent phase still had some way to run. "In ten years' time I'll do my book on Great Train Rides," Kerr added, tongue lolling in his cheek.

The new year was, naturally, crammed full of live bookings, with a European tour set for February. The group went into the studios for some rehearsals in January, and somewhat to their surprise found they'd generated yet another batch of new ideas. One, in particular, kept sitting up and begging for attention, so much so that they decided there and then to have a go at polishing it up and recording it as a single. They were right to back this particular hunch, and they sensed they had a hit record on their hands. The song eventually became 'Promised You A Miracle'.

Kerr recalled, "I thought, if we do have a hit it will be a fluke. We went away and the first tune we got was a riff for 'Miracle', and we just looked at each other and said, 'This is *it*!' We had two days to go before we were to embark on a European tour, and we just rang Virgin and said, 'We've got this song and we want to do it, this is the hit single.'"

Grabbing a few hours of spare studio time and a young

engineer, Peter Walsh, who'd remixed 'Sweat In Bullet' a few months earlier, the Minds banged the song down on tape in one intensive session and were amazed to find that it was finished and ready to go. Kerr: "I remember we were getting the boat to Sweden in about three hours' time and the rest of them had gone, and Charlie and I sat there – Pete Walsh is like nineteen years old – and we sat there with a bag of Treets and a bag of wine gums and it was light coming through outside, and it was just like, everything is possible."

'Promised You A Miracle' was, in a sense, a return to first principles. It was obviously a formally-structured song with verse, bridge and chorus, but on the other hand it was infused with a modern funk feel and a pared-down determination to get straight to the point. Especially gratifying was the way the song breathed between choruses, the musicians audibly pausing to gather their strength for a moment before bearing down hard on the hookline. The song sounded clear and confident, and after a sticky start in the lower reaches of the chart it began to climb rapidly.

The Minds were clattering around France and Belgium as 'Miracle' soared up to number 13 – where its progress was disappointingly halted – but they managed to get back to Britain for an all-important appearance on *Top Of The Pops*. They also found time to deal with some of the requests for interviews which were suddenly pouring in from assorted magazines who'd never paid any attention to the band before.

Kerr found the experience a trifle unsettling. Simple Minds had spent years resolutely ploughing their own singular furrow, and now suddenly they'd taken a long stride towards becoming public property. He wondered if they shouldn't remain more aloof and precious. Was he somehow giving the game away by appearing in the tacky tabloids and the teeny glossies? Doubts were soon dispelled.

"I was halfway through writing the song when I thought, 'This isn't us,'" he said. "Then I thought, 'Hang on a second, *what* isn't us? What a terrible state to have got into if Simple Minds are all tied up in a box and finished.'

"With that single, we've had a few letters from people who

liked us before saying 'you've sold out' blah blah blah. But that's why we've always been honest about our influences. We only formed to play music that we'd heard and liked and to do our own version of it, and to pretend that the only things we've ever liked have been Magazine, the Doors or Roxy Music would be false. We don't get up at half-past eight in the morning and play Joy Division, or I don't. We play Diana Ross, Stevie Wonder and Motown albums, and 'Promised You A Miracle' is every bit as true as our other songs."

CHAPTER 11

With their latest bout of touring completed, the group applied themselves to the next album. To write new material for what would become *New Gold Dream*, the Minds retired to an old farmhouse in the Fife countryside. They'd acquired another drummer by now, Hyslop having departed after a series of personality clashes. The new man was Mike Ogletree, formerly with the ill-fated Cafe Jacques and thus another name from Bruce Findlay's complicated past.

When they got down to work, ideas again flowed readily, assisted by a few rough working cassettes of material generated during the rehearsals in January. They'd already recorded one of those pieces, 'King Is White', for a session for David Jensen's Radio 1 show in February. For the forthcoming album, the piece would be extensively reworked.

Charlie Burchill explained: "For every album we go away to some residential place where you can play the gear at any time of day, and once you start you just get carried right through these things. I've seen us staying up for, like, eighteen hours on an idea that next day we're probably going to think nothing of. It's a great way of learning about writing. You don't have any preconceptions and when you look back you can see all the mistakes and all the good things that happened, which you can then take and use the next time. Things become direct and faster because you've got this knowledge behind you."

They hired Pete Walsh to produce them. Although he was young and his experience to date had consisted mostly of recording soul and funk sessions, Walsh was eager for a chance at a major project and possessed a confidence and sense of purpose way beyond his years. He was swiftly caught up in the group's sleepless lifestyle and monomaniac working processes, but also responded to their passionate determination to achieve the best results possible.

"I was wild and crazy while I was with them," he said, "but I certainly couldn't live like that for the whole year. It does affect you while you're with them, you can't escape it."

"I think we definitely had Walshy right off his nut," Burchill reckoned afterwards. "He was supposed to have stopped smoking and drinking, he was saying to us, 'I very rarely drink,' and all that. At the end of the album he was chain smoking with fucking bottles everywhere."

Walsh had been briefed by Virgin. "Right from the start, Virgin said to me, 'We want the magic and the atmosphere of Simple Minds live to come across on the album, which it's never done before,'" Walsh explained. "I flew out to Belgium to see them playing live just after we'd recorded 'Promised You A Miracle'. I wanted to go for a live drum sound, but not over-the-top heavy metal live – just to try to get a very powerful 3-D sound with all the atmosphere I could muster. So we looked on it as a live studio album, and what felt right to me was something they could go out and gig with straight away, and not have to hire extra musicians to play it with. And I think that came off in their concerts afterwards – apart from the actual compactness of the sound, all the lines that they played live you can hear on the album."

From the start, the basic tracks began to fall into the sort of shape the group wanted, combining a basic uncluttered power with instrumental refinements a further step on from *Sons And Fascination*. Pete Walsh found the writing process absorbing. His own major contributions would not be called for until a later stage, although he made some suggestions. "When they were writing up in Fife, they would jam for two hours on the same song, and then we would listen to it back on cassette, pick the good bits and make the song around that. A lot of it was what they'd call pure shit, or not very good anyway, and there were some magic bits that maybe were never captured on the album."

Another visitor to the so-called "Vibe Factory" in Fife was Jane Henderson, now reconciled to life away from the group. She was impressed by how the band had developed, and noted Kerr's almost-subliminal influence on the writing process.

"I couldn't fault them as musicians and I think they play very well together, but I think Jim is the catalyst. It's not just that he writes the lyrics, but I think he is the spark for all of them. There was a balcony running all the way round this wee farmyard place where they were, and I went up there. It was great watching them, because after a while they didn't realize anybody was there. And Jim would come in and he just perches up in a seat and eggs them on, he's really enthusiastic. He doesn't even need to be singing but he just kind of excites everybody.

"I can't really understand it and it always sounds really pretentious to talk about it, but if he hadn't been there it would have sounded quite clever, but then there's just a kind of magic when they all work together, I think. I like the sort of jargon they've built up through working together, because it's not a musicians' jargon. It refers to colours and moods or the ambience of a film. I think that stops them becoming boring or progressing like Genesis – I think there are similarities with a band like Genesis, but there's this spark that sets them apart."

The *New Gold Dream* material would spawn its own repertoire of working titles and catch-phrases. There were "the Mahler chords" in the instrumental, 'Somebody Up There Likes You', and Burchill's "skyscraper guitar" in 'Colours Fly And Catherine Wheel'. 'New Gold Dream' itself was originally known as 'Festival Riff', 'Someone Somewhere In Summertime' was still referred to as 'Summer Song' long after it had been officially retitled, 'Hunter And The Hunted' was initially 'The Low Song', and 'Colours Fly' went under the working title of 'Arpeggio Song', thanks to MacNeil's synth arpeggios which ran through it.

"I find it very difficult to get away from the working titles," said Pete Walsh. "'New Gold Dream' was originally 'Festival Riff', and it was like a festival – we pictured it as being something like Kraftwerk, motorway music. Up in Fife, once we got a cassette version of it, we recorded it onto the audio channel of a video cassette of Jean-Michel Jarre in China, and it was great watching him doing his concerts in China with 'Festival Riff' coming out."

"Me and Jim will say to each other particular types of chords that we understand by a certain name," said Burchill, "like the Cale Chords. It's like a very fast communication and you build up this vocabulary."

Armed with their demo tapes from Fife, they headed for the Townhouse Studios in London's Shepherd's Bush to begin recording the basic tracks for the songs. Unfortunately, even at this early stage it became clear that Mike Ogletree wasn't the right choice of drummer. His light, jazz-influenced playing style just wasn't heavy or hard-driving enough for the group's music. Fortuitously, Pete Walsh knew just the right man for the job. He'd worked with Mel Gaynor on a variety of previous sessions, and knew he had the right combination of stamina, brute force and technical expertise for Simple Minds.

"We knew we were on to something big, and that's why the Mike Ogletree saga happened," Walsh explained. "I could have put the tracks down with Mike, but we knew there was something special right from the earliest stage, and that it was too good to waste on something that wasn't happening. I've only had that feeling on a few things, where you definitely know you're on to something big."

Gaynor would eventually play on six of the album's nine tracks. After an initial display of over-eagerness which saw him firing off licks, fills and ornaments into any available space on the tapes, Gaynor settled comfortably into the music. His own background had seen him playing soul, funk and heavy metal, which coincidentally happened to be the required ingredients.

Gaynor came from South London, and he'd been to school in Merton Park, alongside two members of Mod revivalists, the Merton Parkas. One of them was keyboards man Mick Talbot, who later formed the Style Council with Paul Weller. Mel left school as fast as possible to get into music, though he'd toyed briefly with the idea of becoming a chef (he still has the figure of a man who enjoys food hugely). He recalled, "I met Pete Walsh when I was doing sessions at Utopia Studios. The first time was with Heaven 17, he called me in to do that, and also the Heatwave album."

Gaynor had played with Mac and Katie Kissoon, Beggar & Co and Tina Charles, and had worked on the road too. He'd been a full-time member of Light Of The World ("owing to big heads and politics, the band split up"), toured with metallists Samson and been to Japan with the Nolan Sisters. He was barely twenty-two, but was already married and planning a family with his wife Marlene. Along with his formidable stockpile of technique and experience, he also brought with him a blunt, pragmatic attitude to making music, which made an almost comical contrast with the semi-mystical abstractions in which Jim or Charlie would often talk.

"Working with the Nolans taught me a lot about sight-reading," he said matter-of-factly. "Some of the nights in Japan it was ridiculous. They'd just throw a score in front of you with about twelve songs, and all their songs are like medleys so you've got to string it together. I managed it all right, though, it's no problem. You had to think twice."

Apart from 'Promised You A Miracle', Gaynor knew nothing about Simple Minds. "I was really quite excited to play with them when Pete called me in. The vibe from the band was like a really close family, even though I was just doing sessions for the album. Their music isn't so much demanding to play, it's just demanding to get the right feel for. I don't think they're real technical musicians as such, they're feel musicians. It takes a little bit of seeking to get the right feel for every tune."

The Glaswegians found Gaynor's broad South London accent hilarious, though they soon stopped ridiculing him when the massively-built drummer demonstrated not only awesome physical strength but a fondness for "slapping necks" when people began to irritate him. For the time being, Mike Ogletree remained – nominally – the group's drummer, but they quietly laid plans to recruit Gaynor on a more permanent basis as soon as his schedule allowed it.

"Mel was playing with Mac and Katie Kissoon when he was sixteen – ridiculous," said Burchill. "He's one of these people

101

who go to the heart of things. They know where their destiny lies or where they would like it to lie and they just go for it full steam. He's a big session man and he charges rates like a session man, but he's definitely got a much more principled view on things. That's what we recognized in him when he played on the album."

Gaynor salvaged what had threatened to become an awkward situation by recording his parts in a mere three days. The band had been seriously considering scrapping the recording sessions if they couldn't get it right. "We were over the moon," said Burchill. "The parts he played were the same as Mike's, but the power and the conviction were there."

Ogletree's failure to deliver the required amount of propulsion seemed to stem partly from a lack of confidence, since nobody doubted his skill. Gaynor commented: "I saw him a long time ago with Cafe Jacques and he was a really good drummer, really confident. Why has he lost the confidence? It doesn't figure out to me, something must have happened." But nobody knew what.

For the next stage in the proceedings, the entire entourage moved up to the Manor studios, in lush green English countryside near Oxford. Like the Townhouse, the Manor is owned by Virgin, who thus seem to have perfected the art of paying their artists with one hand and taking their money back with the other. But the Manor, a rambling old house with a swimming pool, lake, and rooms for billiards and table-tennis, lent itself to the group's working practices. They could record at all hours of the day and night, they could have a break when they felt like it, and the studio was far enough from London to discourage casual visits from record company personnel. Richard Branson would occasionally pop up to spend the weekend in the flat adjoining the Manor with his girlfriend, but his quiet, almost shy manner meant that he trod on nobody's toes.

Pete Walsh wasn't used to working this way, but he came to appreciate its benefits. "One thing which was very important and came out on a few occasions was the actual leisure side of recording, and the Manor was renamed the Leisure Centre when we were there. I can remember saying to Jim, 'I don't know whether this is the best way to record or the worst,' in that whenever we came up against a problem we'd go and have a game of table tennis or a swim or go fishing, and just have fun and then go back in.

"Derek did an interview on a Saturday morning TV programme with Peter Powell, and Derek said, 'We're working on an album; we're playing a lot of tennis.' Peter Powell said are you doing any recording, and Derek said, 'Yeah well, just a bit.' And it was a question of getting the right balance between having fun and getting down to it, and it really worked."

Another personality problem arose which could have had disastrous consequences for the final outcome, and this time it was one which posed a direct challenge to Pete Walsh. During their last American tour, Simple Minds had recruited sound engineer Frank Gallagher, a short but volatile Scotsman. The band had never met an engineer quite like him, and they liked not only his professional ability but also his capacity to act as "vibe man", goading the group on and getting everybody into a fighting frame of mind.

Though the group wanted Pete Walsh as producer, they were worried that his lack of experience could cause problems over the course of a major project which would inevitably impose punishing physical and emotional strains. Gallagher was brought in as back-up man to do any necessary vibing-up of the participants. His last job had been with Talking Heads, so presumably he knew what he was doing. He'd quit when the enlarged *Remain In Light* version of the Heads toured Japan, having failed to see eye to eye with David Byrne over the group's live sound. Gallagher wanted to turn the levels right up and rock the house, but Byrne wasn't convinced.

Gallagherisms had soon entered the lexicon of band stories, and it demanded no imagination to see why he'd been a source of perpetual embarrassment to David Byrne and his chic Manhattan social set. He had no time for Brian Eno, who'd collaborated with Talking Heads on *Remain In Light* and other albums. "Eno couldn't mix a rice pudding," he declared roundly. "The man has smelly feet and he *never* has a cigarette."

At Simple Minds gigs where the audience had, in Frank's

103

view, been insufficiently enthusiastic, he would address the crowd through the PA system as the house lights came up – "thank you for your money and now *fuck off*." When the band were onstage in the middle of a song, Gallagher would threaten them through the onstage monitors. Mick MacNeil recalled one occasion when he'd been appalled to hear an angry Glasgow voice bellowing from the speaker next to him. "MacNeil! Turn down! You're too loud and my reputation is at stake." MacNeil ignored him. The voice came back. "MacNeil! MacNeil! Turn down or you're out of the mix."

Gallagher was notoriously intolerant of journalists, whom he referred to as "pond life". He was intolerant of photographers, whom he would chase away from the band's dressing room with cries of "paparazzi bastards". Occasionally, he was even intolerant of the Minds' material. One day at the Manor, he snatched up the lyric which Kerr had just completed for 'Someone Somewhere In Summertime' and scanned it critically. "Pure art, Kerr," he announced scathingly. "Means nothing to anybody."

However, Gallagher overstepped the mark at the Manor, moving into the lavish master bedroom, generally lording it around the place and giving the impression that he was in charge. In the event, Pete Walsh didn't need any help, and he resented Gallagher's presence hovering behind his left shoulder, waiting for him to foul something up. Finally, by mutual agreement, Gallagher departed abruptly for New York, to everyone's relief. "You need an atmosphere and a good feeling between everyone involved," said Walsh, "which is why Gallagher got the boot, because he was upstaging too many people."

CHAPTER 12

Once in motion, the *Dream* rolled on regardless. With the drummer problem resolved and Walsh firmly in the driving seat, Simple Minds were able to get on with building what would be easily their most accomplished set of songs to date. In some respects, it's the finest record of their career, a creative high-water mark even if later releases would be bigger, brasher and sell far more copies.

"I think we lucked out with *New Gold Dream*," Jim Kerr said in 1987. "It's a one-off. Well, I hope it's not a one-off, but I think it's a one-off of a certain period. You always like to hope that the magic comes and sometimes it just kind of happens and somewhere up the road you're gonna get it again. It's like Van Morrison when he hit *Astral Weeks*, and it's just there."

If parts of *Sons And Fascination* had almost written themselves, *New Gold Dream* was like stumbling into a hitherto unknown dimension. It was "rock music" on the face of it, with pounding beats and big bass riffs, but over and above that the music was shot through with rare melodic grace and delicate emotional nuance. In pieces like 'Hunter And The Hunted' or 'Big Sleep', the group achieved a Mahlerian poignancy, an occasionally Strauss-like opulence. On one occasion, when Walsh was mixing 'Someone Somewhere In Summertime', Burchill burst into tears. The impact of the music played at high volume over the studio's giant super-quality speakers could be overwhelming.

"I remember phoning up Bruce Findlay and saying, 'We've really kinda surpassed what we should be,'" Kerr recollected.

105

"He was going, 'It's two o'clock in the morning, what *are* you rabbiting on about?' and I was just going, 'You don't *understand*!' "

It frightened him, too. "Those backing tracks were just so enormous, I was just really afraid of trying to find a voice and a sentiment that could match them. Inside I knew that I had them but it was just a matter of bringing it out without going over that fine line that divides grandeur from pomposity. Eventually I had one day left and I was just *forced* to do it. I had all these pages with phrases on them and I just formed the structure of the songs as I went along.

"Then, when I came out and I *knew* it had worked it was just a brilliant feeling, but a feeling of danger that you'd attained something that you'd got no right to, you'd reached a point you really shouldn't have reached."

Walsh had done his homework on the group's previous output, analyzing its weaknesses and probing for areas which needed emphasizing or improving. "After hearing all their previous albums, I thought it was time they settled down and got into something vocally a bit more constant, something a bit more obvious, but to try and retain the atmosphere. There were a few occasions where Jim would sing a vocal and there'd be the wrong rhythm in the words and we'd have to chop out a few and perhaps find a new line. I think Jim felt the change in what I was trying to do, and after the first few songs he started to write the lyrics bearing in mind that we were trying to get something a lot more direct. The actual *sound* was the atmosphere, and the words were a lot more meaningful than before, I think.

"Jim also got into the habit of getting one line – 'someone somewhere in summertime' for instance – and would perhaps sing that all the way through the song, and it was a question of saying, 'Right, that should be the chorus there, so sing a chorus and let's work out a verse for that bit.' It was a really good way of working because it was spontaneous, and what felt good at the time got on the record. It was funny that on most of the songs he sang exactly what I thought he would, and it was like all the ideas from the past months had suddenly come together. There was no sort of big decision-making about whether it was the

106

right vocal or not. It happened and it was the best one there was, and it was a good vehicle for the song to work around."

Again, Walsh noted Kerr's influence on the others. "He only put his vocals on at the end, but he was there all the time and was a constant source of inspiration, I think, to the other guys. Not belittling any of the others or anything, but if it was all right with Jim then it was all right with them, you know? Which I think is great, to actually have someone in the band who isn't a dictator, but the others can look across to him and say, 'Well, was that how we were hearing it up in Scotland?' It was the old happy family coming in again.

"On the face of it, they have the aura of being the tiny wee men from Glasgow, but underneath it all there's that strong driving force. They're not the kind of guys who'll come up and yell in your face, but you just know when something's wrong. You know you're on a winner when they're not saying anything. On the surface they do appear to be very easy-going, likeable people, which they are, but underneath there's this desire to do better and better and better and better. I should think that feeling has influenced a lot of their decisions along the way, with regard to changing producers, or whatever."

New Gold Dream was not the kind of record that happens very often, catching the several sides of Simple Minds in a lush cocoon of sound which greatly contributed to the album's sense of completeness. It wasn't a concept album, but the tracks shared the same moods and colours – with the exception of 'Glittering Prize', released as the second single just before the album appeared in September 1982. The track served its purpose, scampering into the Top 20 and bolstering up the group's new-found chart status, but it was the runt of the litter. A few months later, Forbes told Burchill he'd heard a Muzak version of 'Glittering Prize' in a London supermarket. "God," said Charlie, "it's bad enough when we do it."

Elsewhere, you could quibble if that was your preference, but *Dream*'s hypnotic qualities were not easily picked apart. 'Somebody Up There Likes You' was their most guileful instrumental to date, phrasing crabwise across Ogletree's percussion as MacNeil's synths screamed overhead like 747s over Manhattan and Burchill added shadows and overtones. "I've got this thing with Charlie where I think exactly the same as he does," said MacNeil. "If we were in different rooms and we started playing, the end result would be quite the same. There's no melody standing out, no drumbeat. Basically, it's everything flowing together."

MacNeil was especially happy with 'Hunter And The Hunted'. He liked its formal, crafted structure, and he was pleased that they managed to get Herbie Hancock to contribute a synthesizer solo when he paid a visit to London. "I think the song has a certain mood until it comes to that solo, and then it totally changes without any problem," Mick reflected. "It shows you that it doesn't really matter what kind of music you're playing – you can still blend it all together."

In 'New Gold Dream', Ogletree and Gaynor had recorded two drum parts simultaneously at four o'clock one morning, shovelling out a massive backbeat that produced enormous power. "We nailed 'New Gold Dream' right away," Burchill said. "Derek was playing this really fast pumping bass and it meant nothing, and just before that I'd been doing this guitar riff thing and it meant nothing either. Then by accident we put the two together and Jim went off his nut, he went, 'Yeeees! Fucking brilliant!' Then we just went for it right away." Any resemblance to the Velvet Underground's 'What Goes On' may not be entirely coincidental. The track had originally run for ten minutes or more, but Walsh edited out the less inspired sections so that the finished take jumped from peak to peak.

He'd done the same with 'King Is White', and the song sounded entirely different to the Radio 1 version, which had been recorded with a bleak drum machine and a chilly vocal from Kerr. That first attempt at the song had been more in keeping with the source of its inspiration – Kerr had written his lyric after watching reruns of President Sadat's assassination on TV, and the recording had an edgy, sinister quality which wouldn't have been out of place on *Empires And Dance*. The album version introduced an opulent Arabian Nights feel, spice-laden and mirage-like.

Perhaps *New Gold Dream* was too much of a good thing. Some

reviewers loved it ("special and triumphant" – Paul Morley, *NME*), some liked the band's playing but found Kerr's semi-Biblical imagery and visionary zeal too much to cope with, and the occasional oddball despised everything about it. When Brian McGee heard it, he was struck by its sense of sadness. "It brings tears to your eyes," he said. Kerr himself referred to its "coffee table" quality, a remark which perhaps planted the seed in some minds that *Dream* was little more than manicured blandness.

Hugh Jones, who'd engineered *Sons And Fascination*, was one listener who couldn't see what all the fuss was about. "I loathed it. I can be specific, because there were certain things about Simple Minds I really loved, and one of them was their use of keyboards. Keyboards is a really dodgy area because it's either going to be something interesting and original or it's going to be Yes, just weeping sustained chords which personally I don't like. Because it's very easy to do that, to sound impressive just by playing sustained chords on a string synth.

"On *Empires And Dance*, the keyboard sounds weren't slushy at all, they were really tough and I loved that. With *New Gold Dream* it had all been mellowed out. I find it a very sleepy sort of album, it's very drifty."

Pete Walsh was pleased with the finished product, naturally, and wouldn't hesitate to defend it against all-comers. "Their old albums are great but I think they have too many ideas in them," he said. "I always feel that if there is a good idea there you have to make the most of it and put everything around it. I think *New Gold Dream* was three-dimensional. I think the other albums were two-dimensional in that everything was the same level, all the guitar lines sounded like one, and there was no real depth."

Partisanship aside, *New Gold Dream* has stood the test of time comfortably. It's a difficult record to place in a general perspective, because, as Kerr says, it's one of a kind. For the group, the next step was simple – they went back on the road with the new material. First stop was Australia, then it was on to Canada and then back to the UK. Planning tours was simple enough, but the next artistic moves wouldn't be so easy.

109

CANADA

An eyewitness account of life on tour, originally published in Melody Maker, *27 November 1982.*

The land was dull grey-brown and it rolled bitterly away northwards as far as the eye could see. Occasionally we'd pass a line of slope-roofed barns squatting among a thin straggle of trees, or see a station wagon tracing a lonely line between the horizons, lost on the way to nowhere. It was like one of those Edward Hopper paintings, a starkly formal portrait of utter isolation.

It was country like this that inspired Jim Kerr to write 'The American', though, of course, this was Canada. Kerr squinted through the window of the tattered grey tour bus. "It's laughing at us," he said. *"See me as I'm cocooned up in badlands . . ."*

Since the opening night of the tour at Vancouver's Commodore Ballroom, it had been desolate going on the prairies. The omens hadn't been promising from the start. Even before Simple Minds played their first Canadian gig, the truck carrying the PA across the Rockies had collided with another vehicle. The band's road crew had escaped relatively unscathed, but all that remained of the driver of the other truck was a hand. Since then, it had been Calgary, Edmonton and, the night before, Saskatoon – all cowtowns until the last few years, when massive finds of subterranean oil had lured the big corporations to the north west in droves. Suddenly, these outposts in the back of beyond had turned into flourishing cities of concrete and glass, cut by the winds slicing down from the Arctic.

110

In Calgary, a local lad helping shift the group's gear had told me about the teams of crazed volunteers who trekked north to take seismic soundings for more buried oil. They'd set out for three or four months at a time, drilling holes in the frozen earth, dropping dynamite down them and taking readings on their instruments. Then they'd head back into town, collect hefty amounts of money for their efforts, then blow it all on wild nights of drinking and driving and drugs. Then they'd set out again to earn some more.

Nobody was too happy with the tour so far. The promoter hadn't hired enough transport for the equipment or any full-time drivers, so the band's road-crew were faced with hefty cross-country drives on top of their usual duties. Then, after the whole entourage had trailed across miles of chillingly barren country, they found themselves playing to the same small audiences they'd encountered the year before, audiences still unfamiliar with the latest *New Gold Dream* album.

The gigs so far had been good, but – apart from the first two out of three nights in Calgary – unspectacular. Then in Saskatoon, the Minds found themselves playing to a crowd of Halloween revellers dressed as pigs, bears, pirates or Indians. Some had come in full Ku Klux Klan regalia and the band had refused to play until they'd been thrown out. The Minds' performance had taken second place to overheated bouts of mating on the dancefloor, and they'd refused to do an encore.

Backstage, tour promoter Frank Weipert had found himself on the receiving end of a severe tongue-lashing, which he'd accepted with a mournful whipped-spaniel expression.

"For God's sake say something, Frank," snapped an exasperated Jim Kerr, still black-eyed and white-faced with stage make-up. "Tell us if we're wrong, but *say something*."

Weipert said nothing and slunk into a corner. Then the local promoter had come in, dressed as an Indian chief. He'd been released on bail from the police station downtown a couple of hours before, after being busted for possession of cocaine.

"This was supposed to be a 90-minute show," he said menacingly. Bassman Derek Forbes was hearing none of this,

111

and got up to give him the full eyeball-to-eyeball. The promoter retreated with indecent haste.

So here we were on the way to somewhere called Regina, trying to catch up some sleep after a late night in Saskatoon. Mick MacNeil was asleep under his Walkman and airline eye-shade. Charlie Burchill was tossing uncomfortably in his seat, listening to Wendy Carlos playing Bach's Brandenburg Concertos on synthesizer. Derek Forbes had collapsed insensible in the back seat. Drummer Mike Ogletree was up front somewhere with support band Visible Targets, from Seattle.

Lighting man Steve Pollard, according to himself Officially Declared Erotic and six-foot odd of pure sex, was asleep on the floor. He woke up abruptly, slipping automatically into a macho pose even as he rubbed the sleep from his eyes and tried to disentangle his biker boots from under a seat. He looked out of the window and his mouth dropped open in horror.

"Jesus Christ! This whole country looks *exactly the fucking same*. Gimme some fucking *scenery*." He glared fiercely down the bus at tour manager and guru Lenny Love, yet another old acquaintance of Bruce Findlay's who'd once been involved in setting up the Rezillos' Sensible label. "Lenny!" roared Pollard. "Organize some fucking scenery!" Lenny pretended to ignore him. Pollard gave up and folded himself up again on the floor.

By now, Saskatoon had faded into the distance behind us, and for all we knew didn't really exist at all, so complete was the desolation of the prairies. The cramped and rattling bus was too cold and uncomfortable for serious sleeping, and the previous drive to Saskatoon had been an overnighter. Tempers were frayed and nerves were rasping painfully against each other. Nevertheless, I managed to slip off into some semblance of a doze.

I jerked awake again as the bus lurched to a sudden halt. People were clambering to the windows.

"Christ!"

"Oh, fuck!"

"Jeeesus . . ."

I got up and peered out. On the rough grass separating the two lanes of the highway, the bright yellow truck which had been carrying the PA lay on its side, top and sides ripped off, the battered black metal of the engine poking through the remains of the bonnet which had been torn apart like a strip of cardboard. Behind it, the PA was scattered across the ground. At the side of the road, soundman Johnny Ramsay was bent over two prostrate forms under blankets – J-P and Andre, the roadies from Montreal who'd been in the truck. My stomach did a slow somersault, a familiar feeling from forgotten shocks somewhere in the past. We all thought the two casualties were dead.

Some of us got out to help. George, the band's wardrobe man, carried an armful of blankets. Lenny Love got a fast briefing on the situation from Ramsay.

"Help me to lift J-P," barked Ramsay. "I want to get him lying flat."

"You shouldn't move him," said Paul Kerr, Jim's younger brother and chief of the road crew. "He's got to lie flat," said Ramsay, marshalling people round the still and ash-grey figure on the grass. J-P was lifted gently off the ground. I spread a blanket under him on the side of the road. J-P was moaning, saying something about his back. He was lowered to the ground and lay perfectly still, staring at the sky.

The other victim, Andre, seemed in better shape, and was able to lift his head and talk coherently. Meanwhile Pollard and I tucked more blankets round J-P, and Pollard tried to talk reassuringly to him. He didn't answer, just moaned again. His face was covered with tiny cuts, and fragments of gravel were embedded round his mouth. I hadn't seen anybody die before, and I found myself wondering what he'd look like as a corpse. I decided he'd look pretty much the same except his eyes would be closed.

Meanwhile the coach driver was radioing for emergency medical aid. We were miles from anywhere, and as a steel-edged wind ruffled the blankets covering the injured men I thought this had to be the bleakest spot I'd ever seen. I'd been off the bus for about four minutes and my hands were already numb. The sheer *hopelessness* of the scene was a revelation.

There wasn't anything more to be done. A medical kit lay open on the grass, surrounded by wrappers for morphine shots

113

which Johnny Ramsay had pumped into the crash victims as soon as he'd arrived – he'd been following right behind in a U-Haul truck carrying the rest of the band's equipment. All anybody could do now was wait for the ambulance and try to comfort the injured men.

We all got back into the bus. I felt shaken but sucked dry of emotion. I took a final look out of the window at the scene, the two casualties and the pathetically mangled truck with "Demenagez avec RYDER" painted on its front. Big fucking joke. The bus pulled away slowly. "Lenny, let's got home," said Kerr.

Nobody could think of anything to say for a while, then Steve Pollard suddenly erupted. His male-model features were almost comically twisted with anger, and his voice stammered and shook. "It's that b-bastard Frank Weipert's f-fault. We should have had one ar-artic and two full-time drivers. This is the l-last time we cut corners on a tour, it's just not fucking worth the risk . . . this is our third crash this year."

He shook his head, probably remembering the time he'd rolled the truck carrying the Minds' lighting equipment in Belgium back in March. Luckily neither he nor John Ramsay, also in the cab at the time, had been injured.

Kerr, steely-eyed, said, "If that had been my brother in that truck . . ." He clenched his fist slowly. It had been a small glimpse of the precipice, but a remarkably sobering one.

An hour or so later we reached the Relax Inn motel in Regina, and I went looking for a bar with Burchill and Ogletree, determined to get raging drunk. Regina was a sparse collection of low buildings strung around a grid of highways which served as efficient conduits for the probing knives of the wind. The wind is the most memorable thing about this part of Canada.

We found a bar beside a MacDonalds, at the back of a gas station. We worked through a fine assortment of beer, Jack Daniel's and vodka, then decided to have a meal to the accompaniment of a country and western band which had plugged in and started playing for that night's Halloween celebrations – 'Theme From The Beverly Hillbillies', 'Fox On

114

The Run', and the very apt 'Six Days On The Road'. Yee-harrr! Then we headed back to the Relax Inn to find the others.

"Don't worry," said Charlie Burchill. "Those guys'll be okay." Imagine our surprise on looking into the restaurant next to the motel and seeing Andre and J-P, bandaged but fairly cheerful, talking to Ramsay and the support band. The ambulance had taken two hours to reach them, but despite injuries which included busted ribs and a punctured lung they'd been allowed out of hospital after treatment. J-P was due to return for surgery a few days later.

Late that night, Jim Kerr and Lenny Love chewed over the events of the day, and of the tour so far. Clearly, the entire operation left much to be desired. Kerr was uncharacteristically bitter and disillusioned.

"Gigs aren't meant to happen here," he said darkly. "Even cars shouldn't be out here, people shouldn't be out here, let alone bands signed to Virgin Records. I remember when we were out at Rockfield studios for the first time, and we had a day off – I went through to Aberfan where they had that disaster. And you just didn't see anybody who was our age, in a whole day and a whole night. The hills were just fuckin' grinning. It totally threw me, it was like 'don't fuck around'. That's what I mean. You've got to be weird to be doing this in the first place. It's just this part of the country – Vancouver and Montreal are great, but I've never felt so uninspired as I do here.

"If we'd wanted to play stupid places and make money, we should have stayed in Australia. The MD of the record company in Australia told us last year, 'If you stay here for a year and tour, I guarantee you'll be really rich guys at the end of it.' But here, we really are playing for ourselves and a few other people. The most annoying thing about these hick gigs is no matter if you get ten encores, you just don't think you're being understood. At the risk of sounding condescending, you suspect that people in the hall are hearing that sort of volume for the first time or seeing rock lighting for the first time. They just haven't got a clue what you're doing."

Events had forced the band to reassess their approach to touring. They'd been doing too much, without stopping to consider fully whether they were deriving the maximum benefit from their efforts. For instance, had they delayed the Canadian dates by a month, audiences would have had time to absorb the new album and radio stations would have had some opportunity to play cuts from it.

Also, they'd blundered in their choice of promoter. Frank Weipert had handled some small local gigs the year before, but wasn't equipped or experienced enough to tackle a whole Canadian tour. The Minds had pictured him as a kind of Canadian version of Regular Music, who they'd stuck by in Scotland when other bands dismissed them after they reached a certain level of popularity.

"Because of that sort of thing," said Kerr, "and because we know them as people and we know what they go through, we'll always look for the Pete and Barry or the Regular Music in every country we go to. Frank's in that vein – he took us to Canada and gave us four or five dates when nobody else would touch us, so we thought, 'Great, we'll come back and make you some real money,' but he just can't put it on. We tour a lot but we're not fucking Doctor Feelgood, where you can just throw your gear up and everybody will have a good time. We've just turned down the biggest fee in our lives to play New Year's Eve in Glasgow, in our home town, because we're not Rod Stewart, it's not about that."

So that was 30 October 1982, an instructive day for all concerned.

We were in Toronto. There was a bang on the door. "I'll get it," I said to Lenny, who was trying to make sense of lists of figures and a pile of receipts. I opened the door and Kerr walked in, moving rapidly.

He crossed the room, then started doing nervy circuits of the space between the bed and the window. "Lenny, give me a drug of some description," he said to the preoccupied guru. Kerr had spent the day in London, Ontario, doing interviews, while the rest of the entourage was holed up in this Toronto hotel.

On the strength of the crash and the damaged equipment, gigs in Regina, Winnipeg, Guelph and London had immediately

116

been scratched. That left two nights in Ottawa and one each in Montreal and Toronto. The body of opinion in Simple Minds had been all for abandoning the lot and flying straight back to London to prepare for the band's imminent five-week British tour. Unknown to Mike Ogletree, the Minds planned to replace him with Mel Gaynor before the British tour, so rehearsal time was crucial.

The day after the wreck, we flew straight to Toronto with every intention of catching the first flight to London the following day. But driving into the city along brightly-lit freeways, seeing the friendly forest of lights, skyscrapers and the old New York-style grandeur of the Royal York hotel, it had started to feel like a tour again. Why had we been stuck out there in the West when we could have been playing places like *this*? everybody started to think.

Everyone gathered in Kerr's room for a crisis meeting the following day. A change of heart was apparent. "If we can get some assurance that the gigs are well organized, let's do them," said Forbes bluntly. Mick MacNeil agreed. So did Kerr.

That left Charlie Burchill fully geared up to argue the case for leaving Canada, but without a leg to stand on. He was beginning to show the teeth which accounted for his nickname of "Charlie Piranha". "Look, Jim, I just want to know one single thing that's changed to make it worth our while staying."

"Aren't I allowed to change my mind?" demanded Kerr irritably. Burchill, exasperated, ranted for a few minutes, then finally agreed to stay. Meanwhile, Paul Kerr, hugely unmoved by all this drama, was on the phone to room service.

"Yeah, I want tea for nine people, five pieces of cheesecake, four pieces of gateau and some teacakes. I ordered all that half an hour ago and it hasn't arrived yet, so get a move on, willya?" The Canadian Tour '82 was back in business.

After the dark days out West, the Eastern dates were a roaring success, even though a dangerously euphoric Simple Minds fell apart somewhat during their first night in Ottawa. The best night of the tour was unanimously agreed, afterwards, to have been the gig at the Spectrum club in Montreal. Thanks to a van breakdown, coupled with the Minds' usual vague sense of time,

117

it nearly didn't happen at all. At 2 p.m. on the day of the show, I'd been eating a burger with MacNeil in the hotel in Ottawa.

"The record company's just been on the phone from Montreal," he said matter-of-factly. "We're supposed to be doing an interview there half an hour ago." He ordered some tea and a glass of milk and grinned.

The day was saved by a typically galvanic piece of driving by the tour manager and guru (grinding teeth, intense staring eyes and several pedestrians lucky to be alive). This ended with the Wee Men piling out onto a Montreal pavement in front of the Spectrum club only three hours late for soundchecking.

The band scampered inside, and were delighted to find themselves in a large club sporting a sizeable dancefloor ringed with tables, plus a big stage flanked with video screens. After the dark and sterile locales of the prairies, this was (at last) the business. "Tonight, the Wee Men will triumph," trumpeted Kerr gleefully.

Steve "Born To Pose" Pollard was overjoyed because he had plenty of scope to play with his lights. "I am *e-ro-tic!*" he declared loudly, stroking his own leather-clad thigh.

"Faggot," said Paul Kerr, who was passing.

"I'm more man than you'll ever be and more woman than you'll ever have," retorted Pollard disdainfully. Ramsay, nearby, took no notice, but was delighted with the sound. Mostly, the place just felt good and everyone was raring to go.

Fate continued to pull cheap shots right up to the last moment. The cleaners had ripped the shirt Kerr had planned to wear, so he had to borrow one from Forbes. A French-Canadian TV crew crammed the dressing room with gear and interviewed Kerr until two minutes before showtime. Pamela from the support band freaked and barricaded herself in their dressing room. But none of this was allowed to matter.

As the tape of the introductory 'Somebody Up There Likes You' faded, the Minds eased into a tough and resilient '70 Cities As Love Brings The Fall', Forbes' bass driving hard under Burchill's singing guitar harmonics and MacNeil's leviathan wails of synthesizer. The pulse firmly established, they snapped into 'Colours Fly And Catherine Wheel', strung tight across

118

Forbes' thumb-slapped bass riff. At last, it felt as though Simple Minds had shaken off the ghosts which had been stalking them across Canada.

I worked my way round the perimeter of the hall, absorbing the performance, watching reactions. A lot of people danced, some stood and smiled, others appeared entranced. The group were already planning greater things for the British dates, but on a night like this Simple Minds strode easily above all preconceptions or any imagined boundaries.

In 'King Is White', Kerr took the final leap and delivered a vocal performance of true savagery. He'd been working up to this throughout the tour, inserting yells and whoops, ducking sideways and dropping into sudden crouches. Tonight, the recorded version's simple "wire 'em up!" became a stream of hysterical orders: "Wire 'em up – string 'em up – fuck 'em up – *hang* 'em up . . ." Around him, Forbes swooped and swooned on his fretless bass, MacNeil deployed hallucinatory shrouds of synth and Burchill unleashed whiplashes of wah-wah guitar. It was, in short, a night to remember. Or, as Laura from the support band put it, "their music's really *sensual*."

After all this, the final date in Toronto could only be an anti-climax, good as it was. Peter Gabriel and his band, in town for a show of their own the following night, dropped by to enthuse. "You're home and dry," Gabriel told Kerr afterwards.

Somehow nobody missed the plane home, so soon afterwards we were home and dry. The Tour That Nearly Never Was was no more.

119

CHAPTER 14

The group at work, writing and rehearsing new material. A location report.

February 1983: after hours of motorway and threading down country roads across dark snowy countryside, Bruce Findlay and I finally reached the Chapel, in an obscure part of Lincolnshire, around nine. Shadowy trees and black buildings jumped into sudden focus as the car's headlights swung in a wide arc across the drive, and we crunched to a halt.

Simple Minds had been holed up in what now resembled a rural Antarctica for a couple of weeks already, and greeted us like explorers marooned on a glacier who've just spotted a rescue helicopter chucking food parcels at them. Soon, we were huddled round the fire in the pub up the road while the group described the progress they'd made so far. They already had four tracks bashed into reasonable shape, and were confident that more would be forthcoming. Ideas were flowing freely, and there was every reason to expect that they'd leave the Chapel in a further couple of weeks with the best part of an album's worth of new material.

Ideally, they'd have closeted themselves away at Rockfield for this writing session, but the place had been booked up. The Chapel, which belongs to ex-Motor and solo artist Bram Tchaikovsky, had been suggested as a last-minute substitute.

The evening wore on. Pubs in South Thoresby, Lincolnshire, probably never got very full, so the landlord was making the most of this bunch of increasingly rowdy Scotsmen. Kerr, who rarely drinks, was putting away a string of bourbon and cokes. Burchill was advancing his own version of the history of the world, Findlay had started to sing and the author found his wallet was empty. It was plainly time to leave.

Over the next few days, life at the Chapel stumbled along powered by its own eccentric momentum. Since songwriting for Simple Minds meant all of the band getting together to bounce ideas around, it therefore depended on everybody wanting to do it at the same time. Nothing happened for three days.

Kerr hadn't started writing lyrics yet, but this was par for the course since the Minds' writing process invariably meant the other four developing instrumental tracks, then making any necessary adjustments to accommodate Jim's vocal lines. Still, Mick MacNeil wondered if it might not be a good idea to introduce the vocals earlier on in the process.

"You get some really amazing songs that haven't got anything really happening musically, but whatever's playing with the vocal is really good," he said. "I felt we could be missing out on that, where you maybe get a songwriter who sits at the piano and plays and sings along with himself and writes a song that way, where he allows enough spaces for this and that before he starts a vocal, so it's all tied in really tightly with the music. We can't really do that without Jim contributing earlier.

"I think he'll do that more this time. 'Promised You A Miracle' is a good example of when he did – we did it on a Portastudio and he wanted to do a rough vocal on it. He never had any words, but he just wanted to hum a tune on it. He was just going 'la-de-da, la-de-da' and that was really good because you realized how much space the vocal was going to cover and where you could be wasting your time on doing something instrumental."

Mel Gaynor was now becoming fully integrated into the group, having joined up for the British tour before Christmas. Already his input had begun to make itself felt, particularly in the rhythm department where Gaynor had decided that Derek Forbes needed a metaphorical kick up the backside. Gaynor could play a bit of bass too, so he was arguing from a position of strength. Though he was the youngest member of the band,

121

Mel's professional experience made him in some senses the senior musician.

"It's pushing Derek a lot more," he said. "Before, he'd play more or less what he wanted on the track, without another drummer saying, 'No, that's not really happening rhythmically.' He's respecting the fact that someone can swap ideas with him and also appreciate his instrument."

One evening, Kerr sat in the deserted studio and talked about the way Simple Minds had changed over the past year. The studio was cold, and the silence was tinged with the low hum of an electric fire. Kerr's words were sometimes separated by long pauses as he framed the answer to a question.

"Every January and February is the same to me," he said. "We always use January and February to work on new ideas. We never really get around to forming them, so they're always half-baked. I suppose this time last year we'd be doing the same thing as we are now, except that we'd have half the idea for 'King Is White' or something. Now I've finally stopped playing 'New Gold Dream', which is good as well."

He paused and drank some tea. "I'll tell you probably a big difference from last year, more than just outlook," he went on, suddenly more animated. "If you spend any time here you'll see how little time we spend listening to other people's music. Again, I don't know if that's good or bad, but on our last British tour the only things we listened to were Marvin Gaye and Grace Jones, and they were really just for background purposes."

At the same time, Kerr had grown out of many of the elementary prejudices he'd once held about certain types of music or musicians. He'd no longer discriminate against them merely on the grounds that they were old, or American, or people who made pop hits instead of concept albums. He and Burchill had become obsessed, for instance, with Carly Simon's hit 'Why', which they later discovered had been produced by Rodgers and Edwards of Chic. There had been a time when neither Ms Simon nor Chic would have been on the Minds' list of recommended listening.

"Yeah, things can be great, no matter on what ground they stand," he agreed. "It's just that very few people make good

122

international music. There is a British attitude to music that comes through producers, engineers and bands. We get to the stage where we think we're so good, but subconsciously you think, 'Well, at least we're good for wee British lads, anyway.' You go into the studio and do the album, then you come out into the kitchen for a cup of tea and Radio 1's on, and you get the weekly British rock papers, and you take them as though they're worldwide views. It's hard to accept that they only affect Britain to an extent, and in a little way a few other places."

The Minds had always struggled to make headway in Britain, and had found acceptance in Europe and elsewhere before the crowds would turn out for them in Manchester or Oxford. It had given them a less parochial outlook than many of their British peers, and had also given them the courage of their own convictions.

"It's like trying to impress other people less, but trying to make something that impresses us even more," Kerr explained, "and being arrogant enough to accept that whatever impresses us a lot will really knock most people on their backs. On one hand we feel we've come to a real mature stage, a stage that sort of qualifies us in this music we're making, but the other thing we've learned is that the *more* you learn, the more you discover you've got to go."

He went over to the window to illustrate the point. "It's like you've got to get good enough to grow to the height of that window, and once you get to that height you look out and you see an absolute mass, and that's where we are just now.

"You get to about here," he said, indicating a spot a few inches below the window-sill, "and you think, 'Oh yeah, we know it all,' and suddenly your view just explodes overnight. I think by saying that, it means for the first time we genuinely think that for us now the possibilities really are endless. Before, that was just a cliché, it was like saying, 'I don't know.'"

Since *New Gold Dream*, Kerr had sensed a change in attitudes towards the band. "Since that album there's been a certain type of letter coming in that's great. It's from people in a sort of confused state, and they say, 'I'm not a sort of fan or teeny-type person but I just wanted to say that this thing's really good.' It's

123

almost just giving us encouragement, I think, it's not bowing down to us. But obviously on the other side there's the 'What's your birthday? When are you touring?' stuff; the obvious things.

"When I went back to Glasgow recently I spent a lot of time with this girlfriend of mine from a few years back, she used to work with us from the beginning – Jane Henderson. She's great, her and her brother Davey. You know when people are a part of you and then they leave, there's always a certain . . . bitterness isn't really the word, but a sort of ironic truth would come from them.

"When I got back there was this letter from her saying, 'I could just never imagine the band being capable of being anywhere near as good as they are just now.' That was after *New Gold Dream*. And then a follow-up letter from seeing us play a few times on the tour. As I say, their truths are always ironic. These points of view are always really important to us."

New Gold Dream had brought a new level of commercial success, too. Jim and his brother Paul got together and bought a house in one of Glasgow's more affluent suburbs.

"We haven't got enough money yet to buy anything outright, but I've got too much money in my pockets. So where am I gonna keep it? Everyone said buy a house, so I spent a week looking at houses in the price range. I just saw this place and I really liked it, and it's big enough for my parents to stay there and it's big enough for friends coming to Glasgow. Maybe it also gives me a sense of discipline too.

"I imagined that if I ever had the money to buy a house I would buy it in a somewhat more exotic place, but I think that's a very working class attitude, like suddenly you get a little break and think you're nouveau-riche and buy a house in France or Spain or somewhere, or even, for that matter, in the posh district of Glasgow. My youngest brother Mark can still go to school and my mother can still work in the shop. It's too tempting to go to these areas of Glasgow where the nouveau-riche go. I'm not telling you what the price was on tape – it's frightening, Rod Stewart material."

Experiences like the potentially disastrous Canadian tour had forced Kerr and the band to look more closely at the way they worked. As much as they loved touring, it was clear that nobody could maintain the pace they'd set over the previous couple of years, especially when all the roadwork didn't necessarily translate into more records sold or bigger audiences. Much more of this and Brian McGee might not be the only casualty. Bruce Findlay had been all for sending them out on a fifty-date American tour after they'd been round Britain the last time, but Kerr had vetoed the idea. The band were writing new material in Lincolnshire instead.

"It was the end of a two-and-a-half year period for us when we never had more than ten days to two weeks off," Kerr reflected. "Even then they were really rare periods. I think Charlie and I especially thought you can do it all and it doesn't catch up with you. But it does catch up with you, and you're so out of it you blame everything else apart from yourself. That's what we were doing – saying everyone else is responsible for the state of affairs apart from us. But one makes one's bed and one lies in it. I think we know that for everything you do, you pay. It doesn't matter *how* you pay, it's like, 'I'm gonna get more done if I do what suits me best just now.'

"But that Canadian tour – these are the kinds of things where in two years' time we'll be saying, 'Wasn't that a great time, a great tour?' Somebody even said that the other night, looking at all the dates for our next tour in Europe – 'Remember that time we were all in the van, wasn't that a great laugh?' I said, 'Was it fuck, it was horrible at the time. McGee was crying and stuff, it was fucking disgusting and already two years on we're saying what a good time it was.' It was absolutely awful."

Kerr chortled. "I'm not trying to say I feel older or any the wiser, because I'm sure in two weeks' time we'll be back to our old form. But I'm twenty-four this year, and for the first time it feels like we're getting on. Almost overnight it seems to happen, doesn't it, attitude-wise? If you had said to me something about buying a house last October, I might have just laughed at you."

The Chapel's non-productive days straggled past in disconnected bits. Mick MacNeil might get up early and spend a few hours in the studio working on drum machine patterns or keyboard sounds, while the others snoozed on into the afternoon. MacNeil's methodical, mathematical mind is bound to find him producing other artists one day. "It would be good to produce a band, I think," he pondered. "And I'd love to do the sound for a really good live band."

Mel Gaynor, still not attuned to the Minds' bewildering capacity for either sleeping a great deal or not sleeping at all, liked to get up and drive into town in his Ford Granada, roaring off under the sharp winter sky in a belch of exhaust smoke. "They tend to get up too late for me," he grunted, on his way out one morning.

Domestic arrangements at the Chapel were not altogether suited to the group's lifestyle. Bram Tchaikovsky's parents would appear regularly around lunchtime to prepare the evening meal, which implied the sort of homely routine which was exactly what the Minds didn't want. Bram's father was a talkative Yorkshireman with an opinion about everything, a man unused to systematic subversion of the God-given order of things where days start in the morning and end at night. Jim Kerr christened him the Bhagwan.

The group compromised with the family as gallantly as they could. This meant ignoring them by spending the afternoon and early evening listening to the demos they'd recorded or watching TV. Sometimes, the morale-sapping sense of aimlessness was relieved by a visit to the pub up the road, but this option was severely curtailed by lack of funds. Findlay had failed to have the wages sent down from Edinburgh on the appointed day, and so became the object of much heartfelt abuse.

Petty tensions like these can build up, like in movies about submarines trapped on the sea-bed when somebody's personal mannerisms suddenly cause a major emotional flare-up. The Minds had spent too much time together to allow this to happen, although MacNeil could occasionally be heard grumbling that it was "like living with your fucking *grandmother*". Forbes let off steam by borrowing the household's air-rifle and filling tin cans with holes.

On the fourth day the creative drought broke. Money had arrived from north of the border, allowing the group to unwind over a few drinks. By midnight, people had started drifting into the studio. MacNeil was there first, methodically assembling keyboard lines over a rhythm track. With his few days' growth of beard and heavy fisherman's sweater, MacNeil had begun to revert to Hebridean type.

By now, Forbes and Burchill had come to join in. Forbes picked up a bass and began to play over the electronic bassline emanating from one of MacNeil's machines. Burchill strapped on his new Stratocaster, then started to experiment with his echo unit and bank of foot-pedals until he found a sound he felt comfortable with. He began to stroke a few exploratory chord shapes over MacNeil's whiplashing riff.

The door thumped open and Gaynor shambled in. He adjusted some cymbals overhanging his giant drumkit, then sat, head in hand, listening. He occasionally raised an eyebrow to register a question-mark at a change of key or rhythmic shift. Abruptly, he snapped into a crisp drum pattern. Meanwhile, MacNeil began to squeeze out vividly-coloured keyboard textures, from deep growls and roars through 'Miracle'-type piano to piercing trebly shrieks. It was like feeding time in some bizarre electronic menagerie.

A couple of hours had already slipped by. There was no apparent aim in sight, just a sense that the group were feeling their way into something, were still on the upward climb of the parabola. The music hardened gradually, developing from simple riff-with-variations into recognizable sequences with built-in cues and breathing spaces. Forbes began to fashion a further variation on the bassline, working out a tricky chord change with Charlie by nodding and mouthing at him as they kept playing. Gaynor swiftly made appropriate adjustments to his drum pattern, emphasizing the improvements and cueing in returns to the established sequences.

With the groundwork established, something clicked. Melodic lines, hitherto vague, became tightly focused, and an underlying shape began to reveal itself. Perhaps this had something to do with the presence of Jim Kerr, who'd slipped quietly into the studio and was now sitting by the fire, watching with his usual immobility, eyes narrowed and head tilted slightly back. Next to him was a big notebook and a pen, and when an idea sparked out at him from the music he'd write it down in his large, laborious handwriting.

As the four musicians travelled on, by now oblivious to their surroundings, Kerr appeared at my side. "At last we're becoming a *real* band," he said, smiling with secret amusement. He glanced over at Forbes who was standing in front of his amplifier, eyes half closed, jerking from the knees as he pumped out an endlessly wheeling bass figure. Earlier in the evening, Derek had found himself on the receiving end of a tirade from Burchill, who'd felt Forbes wasn't trying hard enough.

"Charlie was really hammering Derek about his playing," said Kerr, half-turning away from him. "Forbes took it right on the chin – it was really good." As the band continued to focus on turning imagination into audible co-ordinates, Kerr hurried back to his pen and notebook to frame another image from this racing picture-show.

Time became meaningless. The studio had lost its identity as an old church full of equipment, and had become instead a collective state of mind. A tragic-looking grey dawn had begun to trickle in at the windows. Around five, Mel and Derek took a break. MacNeil and Burchill gave no sign of having noticed, Mick still juggling riffs and different keyboard sounds, Charlie continuing to explore new chord shapes, shortening and lengthening echo speeds, firing off singing clusters of harmonics. As usual, Burchill seemed to be smiling despite the deepening shadows under his eyes and the faint smear of stubble collecting around his chin.

It was 12.25 p.m., twelve hours since the band had started playing. With the endless circling of sounds, passing and re-passing in different sequences and ordered each time by a subtly different logic, the music had imposed its own shape and meaning on the passing of time. I went to the kitchen to make some tea. As I opened the studio door the hard winter daylight went off in my face like a flare.

Back in the studio, Kerr stood watching MacNeil. Above the thin wisp of beard blurring his jawline, MacNeil's eyes were sunken and utterly driven. He'd jammed another cigarette

128

between compressed lips, but his eyes remained immune to the smoke. "I think MacNeil may be in league with the devil," muttered Kerr.

Mick showed no sign of ever stopping, but he seemed somehow certain of the outcome too. His mind had already passed the finishing tape, and now it was simply a question of forcing his body to go through the motions required for it to catch up. Months later, the track they were working on would become 'The Book Of Brilliant Things'.

That evening, everybody sat round the fire in the living room listening to tapes of what had gone on during the night. Nobody said much, but they just kept playing the sections they were most pleased with over and over. MacNeil leaned back in the sofa, fingering his chin absently. Burchill sat hunched forward, cradling a cup of tea. Kerr stood next to the fireplace, gazing out at the falling darkness and the snowflakes whirling against the windows. I think they were pleased.

CHAPTER 15

Despite Kerr's words of wisdom, 1983 was just as packed with touring as the previous year. First stop was Europe in March. After a string of sunny, hectic shows in Italy, the Minds found themselves grinding up the damp grey autobahns of Germany. The weather probably contributed, but the shows were drab and overcast too.

They played at the Deutsches Museum in Munich one night. The hall was a large square mausoleum full of pillars and mock-classical scrollwork, teetering on the edge of kitsch. Normally, this would be where the stolid local burghers would gather to listen to a little Haydn or Beethoven, and the gloom of centuries hung over the place. The band's spirits were not improved by the knowledge that the hall was only half full. All you could really say about the show was that the group functioned for an hour and ten minutes.

A tall, bearded man wearing an anorak approached Steve Pollard at the lighting desk, and informed him in clipped, efficient English that the show had been *too short*. "Pat Metheny played here for sree-und-a-quarter hours, *vizoud a break!*" he said sternly. It sounded like a fate worse than death. Pollard grunted something ending in "asshole".

He had a point, though. The show had been short, and not very good. Meanwhile, the band had locked themselves away in their dressing room for a post-mortem. They emerged much later, their faces like thunder.

They weren't the only ones suffering from thin attendances, since ticket sales were depressed across the board. Orchestral

Manoeuvres In The Dark had just scrapped a planned German tour for this very reason. But the group weren't helping themselves or their audiences by playing essentially the same set they'd been doing since the previous autumn. They'd made a couple of substitutions and fiddled about with the running order, but it was still *New Gold Dream* with a few trimmings. There were no new songs, and the only variation in the encores was whether they played one or two – or none, on a bad night.

The whole operation was beginning to look like hard work. Obviously, the ambitious two-part show including music from their whole career which Mick MacNeil had sometimes talked about was as far from coming to fruition as ever. It transpired later that Mick had been suffering from a painful undiagnosed stomach ailment throughout this period, which he'd characteristically kept quiet about. The long-term strain was beginning to take its toll.

They polished off the German dates listlessly, then made a brief detour through Scandinavia before heading for the States and Canada again. The American shows were apparently a mixed bag, with some wonderful nights in San Francisco, Los Angeles and New York interspersed with less rewarding shows in the south and the mid-west.

Kerr must have begun to suspect there was bad karma in the air when he was attacked outside the hotel where the band were staying in New York. His assailant was the jealous boyfriend of a girl who was a committed fan of the Minds, and she'd been round to the hotel to meet them. The boyfriend evidently suspected that she'd been doing more than just talking. Kerr was taken by surprise and suffered a broken nose, but this only roused the old Glasgow fighting spirit. By the time members of the band's road crew separated the two, Kerr had inflicted cracked ribs and black eyes on his attacker.

But if Kerr could still find reserves of strength, symptoms of a band at the end of its tether kept recurring among other members of the touring party. Steve Pollard suddenly keeled over in New York with a collapsed lung, while guitar roadie Andy Battye had to be carried unconscious out of a club.

Even the apparently indestructible Charlie Burchill succumbed

131

to a full-scale stress attack. Burchill's frenetic pace of living finally caught up with him, a combination of lack of sleep, hyperactivity and a lethal mixture of drinks triggering a bout of hysterics in his hotel room in the early hours of one morning. Kerr, alerted by crashing and banging noises from Burchill's room which adjoined his own, burst in to find the guitarist apparently trying to force open a window. He looked as though he wanted to jump out, but Kerr managed to prevent him. It was beginning to dawn on everyone that a rest might be a good idea, before somebody died.

The group had to come to terms with their growing status and the different demands it placed on them. It was no longer enough just to go out and play every night – supply had to be geared to rising demand, and delivered where it would do the most long-term good. There were compensations, nonetheless. They were given a heroes' welcome in Toronto and Montreal, cementing the goodwill they'd earned by sticking it out in Canada the year before.

They had a string of festival dates in Europe scheduled for that summer, but before embarking on those the group wisely took a holiday. Charlie and Jim picked up where they'd left off years before, and set off for India together. They saw poverty and filth, and cleared their heads by going walking in the hills. The trip was a way of restoring the close contact the pair had always enjoyed, but which had begun to be worn away by the band's pulverizing schedule. The rest of the group were less ambitious, and returned from a couple of weeks in assorted Mediterranean resorts looking suntanned, for the first time in living memory.

Playing in the open air before giant crowds across Europe during those summer months, Simple Minds felt regenerated. A different kind of power started to emerge in their music, a more basic, rock-weighted feel. The difference was visible, too. Kerr no longer bothered with his livid white face make-up, and he'd washed the black dye out of his hair so it had reverted to its natural brown. Whatever they had to say would be in the music.

"Those gigs brought us back to the rawest kind of state, I think," estimated Kerr. "Some nights it was really rough and a couple of the crew were slagging us off, but . . . ha! But they also knew that it was the best sort of feeling. In places like that, 50,000 people, there's just no room for subtlety, and there's no need for it, there's no want for it."

En route, at festivals like Torhout-Werchter in Belgium, the Minds came into contact with Dublin quartet U2 for the first time. Both groups felt an immediate sympathy with each other, each recognizing shared qualities in the other's music even if U2's spectacular performances were in marked contrast to the Minds' cool control. Their backgrounds were similar, too. Glasgow and Dublin were two cities riven by religious sectarianism and its consequences, and U2 and Simple Minds had both had to look beyond the tunnel vision of their own backyards to realize their ambitions and aspirations. Burchill and U2's guitarist The Edge spent time comparing notes, while Kerr and Bono rapidly struck up a rapport.

"I think we saw a lot of ourselves in them and vice versa," said Kerr later. "We get this thing levelled at us of being influenced by them, but they're equally influenced by us. It might be in a much subtler sense, in dynamics or in some of the sounds. We met at a stage where they had been to America and they had this thing . . . up until then the big kind of people's bands were the Clash and Paul Weller and stuff like that. We felt, 'Fuck them, they're not people bands at all, they're London bands'. They're not international, they're not even worldly, and we have that quality inside us, inherent and boiling."

"I think we saw a confidence in U2 that was inspiring. You're self-aware to an extent, but there's a whole side of you where you don't actually know how you tick and how you work and why it is. It's just there and you get on with it, and then somebody points it out and you come outside yourself and see what they're seeing."

U2 had provided Simple Minds with a practical demonstration of where their own aspirations could lead them. Up until then their potential had existed in part only in their own – particularly Kerr's – imaginations. U2 demonstrated the leap Simple Minds needed to make, but also reassured them that they were capable of it. This was a revelation which would have the most far-reaching consequences.

Kerr said at the time, "The great thing is that we all take it too fucking seriously, and that's the way it really should be. You *should* take it too seriously, because it's a fucking event."

Talk in the music press began to centre on the "new rock" movement being created by Simple Minds, U2, Echo and the Bunnymen and Big Country, a slender theory to start with and one which began to look increasingly frail the more it was reiterated.

Kerr had little patience with it. "I just don't think it exists," he said tersely. "I think it's convenient. I accept it inasmuch as it's probably true, reading between the lines, that we share the same dream. But there's a huge fucking difference between saying you're the best band in the world and *being* the best band in the world." Perhaps he had the Bunnymen's Ian McCulloch in mind here. If so, Mac would wreak a terrible vengeance with multiple slaggings-off of Kerr and Bono in the press in the months to come.

At any rate, it was no great surprise when Simple Minds were invited to appear as "special guests" of U2 at their all-day event at Dublin's Phoenix Park in August, along with Eurythmics and Big Country. "None of these bands is ordinary, I don't think," said Kerr. "There's some sort of magic in there because the end result is so much better than it should be." There was no mistaking the optimism in his tone. It was clear, by now, that Simple Minds were in it for the long run, and that it was only a matter of time before they achieved success on the broadest scale.

The home crowd at Phoenix Park was utterly gung-ho for homecoming heroes U2, who played a garish, metallic set to a non-stop soundtrack of screaming and chanting. Bono, never a man to hold back in front of a crowd, dutifully climbed the PA and paraded around the stage with a white flag, gestures which were beginning to turn into predictable U2 rituals. Sensibly, they later abandoned them.

Earlier, Simple Minds had played under a brilliant blue sky and turned in a towering performance, building steadily and systematically to a climax and including the brand new 'Waterfront', hastily written a few days earlier from an original riff by Derek Forbes. The song's throbbing pulse and enormous sense of space suggested the way the band were thinking (though in a lax moment, Kerr said it made him think of Status Quo). The elaborate, almost ornate arrangements of *New Gold Dream* were receding into the distance. Simple Minds were making bigger music for bigger occasions.

It was album time again. Finally, Simple Minds opted to work with producer Steve Lillywhite, who'd wanted to produce them for some time. They'd begun discussions with Alex Sadkin, the wizard of Compass Point, since they'd liked the sounds he'd been getting with Grace Jones and others, but their respective schedules couldn't be made to fit together.

The choice of Lillywhite may have been symptomatic of the long-term influence of U2, since he'd produced the Irishmen's first three albums, most recently the successful *War*. He'd also been called in to salvage Big Country's debut album, *The Crossing*, after Chris Thomas had been unable to make head nor tail of Stuart Adamson's guitar-heavy version of the Highland Fling. Typecasting was inevitable. Simple Minds conveniently completed a Celtic triumvirate with U2 and Big Country, while Lillywhite became known as the man behind the "new rock" sound.

But doing big rock albums was a relatively recent departure for Lillywhite. His background had included work with a broad variety of artists, and he'd been involved with some innovative records which had broken new ground in their time. He'd worked his way up from being a humble tape-op at Phonogram Studios in London in the early seventies (the studios were later bought by Paul Weller and renamed Solid Bond) to being the in-house producer for Island Records at their studios in St Peter's Square. Then he worked with Siouxsie and the Banshees, and did 'Sound Of The Suburbs', 'Offshore Banking Business' and the *At The Chelsea Nightclub* album with the Members (with whom his brother played drums). "That got me in with Virgin," he said, "who then offered me XTC, with whom I did *Drums And Wires* and later on *Black Sea*."

It was a red letter day when, out of the blue, he was offered the chance to work with Peter Gabriel on his third solo album. "I thought it was one of my mates phoning up as a joke, like, 'Why would Peter Gabriel want me to work with him?' But no, it was true. That was the longest LP I've ever done in terms of time taken, because it was done with lots of gaps. I remember whipping off and doing a Psychedelic Furs record in between.''

Lillywhite was especially struck by Gabriel's willingness to experiment in the studio. ''The crazier the idea the more he liked it. Everything you'd wanted to try but everyone had always said 'oh no, you can't do that', with Gabriel it was 'that's fine, but do *more* of it'. Which is a brilliant attitude to learn, because on records sometimes you've got to be a bit larger than life.''

The group headed for Rockfield for three weeks to work on new songs, and Lillywhite joined them there for the last fortnight. He wanted to familiarize himself with the musicians and the material, and also lobbed a few suggestions into the pot. The band already had half a dozen tracks from the Chapel sessions at the beginning of the year, as well as some new demos they'd made at Nomis in London before the Phoenix Park show.

Little of the raw material emerged from Rockfield unchanged. Arrangements inevitably developed in unforeseen directions as the group became more comfortable with the songs, which had often started life as demos by Mick and Charlie accompanied by drum and bass machines. Also, by now, Mel Gaynor was very much part of the unit, not just a session man hired to play some drum parts as he had been on *New Gold Dream*. His experience and influences began to filter into the songwriting.

''I think on the last album I was stifled a bit because they were telling me what to play,'' he said. ''On this album I'm getting quite a few of my ideas across, not only in the drumming field but in other fields as well. It's a lot different from *New Gold Dream*, both soundwise and material-wise. The last one was very smooth, very polished. This album's got a bit more dirt in it.''

Most of the basic tracks were radically reworked. Often, the components would be stripped down, cut up and pasted back together in an entirely new configuration, perhaps retaining only a bassline or a keyboard melody from the original four-track demo. By October, they'd sorted out the material they wanted to record and were hard at work at the Townhouse again.

Lillywhite brought a practical enthusiasm to recording which chimed with Simple Minds' mood. Where Pete Walsh had been the technician, the perfectionist, Lillywhite would opt to go with the feel of the moment and worry about needles flickering into the red later. He hadn't entered into the project with any great preconceptions about how he wanted the album to turn out.

"I can't say I've sat down and analyzed all their previous recordings to try and find hidden insight into how it should go," he said drily. "I never do that anyway. I knew Charlie was a good guitar player and I wanted to bring him out a bit more, and Mel's a great drummer so you know you can get really good sounds from him. Essentially they're a great *band*. That's what I do like about groups, where no individual member is absolutely outstanding but the whole thing works as a sum of its parts. They're far more democratic in those terms than other groups I've worked with. With U2, for example, Bono is pretty much at the helm."

He also pushed Kerr to write some lyrics earlier on in the proceedings than usual, and to try to record a vocal as soon as possible. Kerr was taken aback one day when Lillywhite suddenly turned to him and suggested he have a go at a vocal take there and then for 'The Book Of Brilliant Things'. "But I haven't written any lyrics," the singer protested. "Well, can you have lyrics in twenty minutes?" riposted Lillywhite sharply. Kerr did.

"It means he gets a shot at it and he can go away and think about it and then have another shot at it and keep upgrading the vocals," explained the producer. "A lot of the vocals you hear on the record are probably done on separate days, even within a song." Thus, he hoped, the time-honoured routine of the band perfecting more or less finished instrumental tracks over which Kerr would eventually sing could be subverted.

"On their earlier records, everyone's parts didn't really bear much resemblance to everyone else's," Lillywhite noted. "Mick would be fiddling away like this, Charlie would be going like this, then Jim would come in and sing something completely different to what the other two were doing. Whereas now I think Jim is taking some of the melodies from the guitar and the keyboards, which he didn't use to, which makes it more like a song."

CHAPTER 16

Nobody has yet managed to come up with a useful portable definition of what a record producer actually does, once you take away the duties performed by tape operators and engineers. Clearly a large part of the job comes down to meeting deadlines and budgets while begging, urging or beating the best possible performances from the artists. A producer must find a delicate balance between authority and comradeship, weighing discipline against artistic licence. Other useful credentials might be monkish asceticism and an ability to concentrate for long periods, the capacity to function without sleep, and paranormal hearing. Nobody said it was easy.

Perhaps you could liken a record producer's role to that of a film director. When the Minds submerged themselves in the Townhouse to begin recording, Charlie Burchill was evidently thinking along the same lines when he chalked "Herzog" on the back of Lillywhite's chair in the control room. Ever since Kerr and Burchill had been to see Herzog's film *Fitzcarraldo*, in which Klaus Kinski brings opera to the Indians in the South American jungle, they'd been fond of quoting the line "only the dreamers move mountains". Kerr had even quite liked the idea of persuading Herzog to take a break from his soccer training with Bayern Munich to produce the band. A picture of Nastassia Kinski was pinned up on the wall to provide inspiration of a different kind.

Without actually living in the studio, it's difficult to keep track of the progress of an LP as it proceeds agonizingly from the recording of basic rhythm tracks through to vocals, final overdubs and general nit-picking. You'd have to be very patient indeed to get to hear an entire track in the course of an evening.

You might walk in to find MacNeil perched behind a synthesizer propped up on the mixing desk, filling in a melody line for the track playing in his headphones while Lillywhite explored levels and balances. There'd be Mel Gaynor out in the studio dropping in a few embellishments to a drum track, or Forbes might have hit upon an idea for an additional bass overdub. Meanwhile, a shifting cast of characters would be playing musical chairs around the control room's soft leather sofas. There would be assorted Simple Minds, Paul Kerr, Simon Draper from Virgin or various acquaintances and girlfriends. Occasionally Lillywhite threw everybody out so he could have a bit of peace and quiet while he tackled a mix.

Time ceases to exist in the normal way inside a recording studio. Supposedly, there are artists who treat recording like a nine to five job, but Simple Minds rarely seemed to hit their stride before four in the morning, usually stumbling out into the daylight around eleven. Time appears to have been transferred onto tape and looped. The same thing happens over and over again with numbing repetitiveness as a track is built up, modified, honed, sharpened and finally completed. It's excruciatingly dull or endlessly hypnotic, depending on your frame of mind. At least the band can come and go when they feel like it, unless they're actually required to record a part. For the producer, manning the console for endless hours at a time, cases of Fader Wrist or VDU Eye are common.

Late one Saturday night, Kerr was revving himself up to sing a vocal for 'Up On The Catwalk'. The earlier part of the evening had been taken up with keyboard overdubs for 'Speed Your Love To Me'. While MacNeil had pensively worked his way through a string of Dunhills and a few shots of Bailey's Irish Cream to steady his hands, Burchill huddled in an adjoining cubicle buried under a pair of headphones, building up a dense mesh of guitar tracks on a Portastudio which would, in the fullness of time, be transferred onto the track in progress.

During the preceding week, the Minds had been working themselves determinedly into the state which still seemed to suit

139

them best. The clear eyes and suntans of a few weeks before had already vanished, though Forbes appeared fairly healthy. MacNeil, on the other hand, looked gaunt and pale, Burchill was cheerful but clearly distracted by some three-dimensional musical brain-teaser nagging away inside his head, while Mel Gaynor made only fleeting visits to the control room, saying little and looking tense.

A couple of days before, Kerr had sat in the control room to watch the others at work. Then, he'd been attentive and relaxed. Tonight, though, he was a coiled spring, nervously shifting chairs, putting on his jacket and taking it off again, jumping up to make tea, occasionally aiming vicious kung-fu kicks at passers-by which didn't miss by much.

"Can you play table tennis?" he asked me suddenly, knowing very well I could but not as well as him. Obviously he wanted to beat somebody at something before getting to grips with the microphone. We adjourned to the table-tennis room upstairs, Kerr skipping ahead down the densely-carpeted, yellow-lit corridors. Despite the author's unplayable forehand smashes, Kerr emerged a convincing winner.

We went back into the control room. Kerr vanished into the dimly-lit spaces of the studio and slipped on his headphones, after clarifying for Lillywhite a few details of which version of the lyrics he was about to sing. Lillywhite, chain-smoking Silk Cuts, ordered Croydon, the tape-op, to find the start of the track. Croydon spun the giant reels of tape back to the zero mark, but was swiftly rebuked by the impatient producer. "Croydon, you should know by now that the track doesn't start there," Lillywhite snapped. "The lead-in runs to at least twelve." Croydon made a gesture which Lillywhite fortunately didn't spot. He was bouncing up and down in his seat and wanted to press on, fast.

"Okay, let's try one, shall we?" he said, and rolled the tape. The track erupted through the powerful studio speakers in a cascade of percussion and piano chords. I hadn't heard it before, and the force of the playing heard at this volume was something of a revelation. Forbes and Gaynor had combined to generate a steamrolling rhythm track which came hammering out of the opening chorus like a runaway train.

140

Some nights, it would take some time before a vocal began to approach the desired spot, but tonight Kerr was immediately on target, punching home the "get out of Bombay, go up to Brixton" line with much drama. "Brixton" had originally been "Britain", but Lillywhite hadn't heard it properly. Kerr preferred Lillywhite's version and kept it in.

Kerr finished a couple of complete run-throughs, then came out of the studio to listen to a playback. Lillywhite indicated the bits he was happy with and made a few suggestions about phrasing and intonation. He was beginning to store alternative vocal takes on separate recording tracks, and when he had enough pieces he liked scattered around the multitrack he would sift through, piecing together a single finished track from the best bits of each version.

Lillywhite suggested Kerr should throw in a few more names towards the end of the song, since he'd been running out of steam as the track thundered to a close. The Minds bandied about a few possible inclusions – Edward Hatspace (a code-name for Bruce Findlay), Simone De Beauvoir, even Tony Hadley (Spandau Ballet's light-operatic vocalist). Luckily these weren't necessary, since Kerr had a couple of spare lines jotted down in his notebooks which were swiftly pressed into service.

Kerr went back into the studio for another shot at it. The track roared into life once more, and as Kerr charged confidently into the first verse Lillywhite visibly lit up with glee, twisting round in his seat to exchange manic grins of triumph with anyone who was watching. Around the control room, ears began to prick up as it became clear that this take was a hot one. Forbes put down the drawing pad in which he'd been sketching the latest adventures of Dan Yer Man and began to nod intently. Burchill was pounding a clenched fist on his thigh. MacNeil, undemonstrative as ever, swayed approvingly.

With the basic shape of the vocal established, Lillywhite began to weed out small mistakes in phrasing and pitch, cueing Kerr in and out systematically as he worked through his shopping list of details.

"Jim, in that second chorus, when you sing the second line

can you maybe vary the melody slightly? I don't think you need to go down to that bottom note each time."

"Okay," said Kerr.

After a mere half-hour, Lillywhite had everything he needed. "Right," he said, "I think we've got it." Kerr emerged from the studio suppressing a triumphant smirk and raised a fist, goal-scorer style. "Bring me East Germany," he ordered cryptically.

"Quick game of table-tennis?" Lillywhite asked him. Kerr, still racing hard on studio energy, agreed. Despite his mastery of devious Oriental backspin and capacity for spoon-bending serves, Lillywhite swiftly joined me on the scrap-heap after a two-nil defeat. He left the room looking disconcerted, and went to cheer himself up with enormous portions of takeaway crispy duck. Kerr flung open a window and acknowledged the cheers of an imaginary crowd of thousands.

CHAPTER 17

The group decided to delay the release of the new album until early in 1984. They could have rushed it out for Christmas, but that would have made a simultaneous worldwide release impossible. It was eventually named *Sparkle In The Rain* after going under the working title of *Quiet Night Of The White Hot Day*. Kerr had promised that it would be "an art record – art without tears with masses of muscle", and *Sparkle* was a densely-packed juggernaut of an LP.

'Waterfront' had been released as a single the previous November, and had reached number 13 in Britain, a level above which some higher authority had evidently decreed Simple Minds' singles should not rise. The group had been up to Glasgow to shoot an accompanying video, and they staged a free concert at Barrowlands Ballroom to get some live footage. Barrowlands, in Glasgow's old market district the Barras, had once hosted the pop package shows of the sixties but had lain derelict for years. It was still tainted locally by memories of the notorious rapist and strangler Bible John, who picked up his victims at the dancehall and recited from the Bible while murdering them. The Minds' appearance inaugurated a new era for Barrowlands as a regular venue for touring bands.

Simple Minds wanted to return to Glasgow for the video-shoot because Kerr had had the city's old docks in mind when he wrote his lyric. "I walked right along the front, and Glasgow was packed with empty ships, like ghost ships. Even from the factories you could hear from the echoes and the acoustics that they were all empty, just shells. And it was kind of special for me because all my people, my grandfather and that, worked on that front. So I was looking about and there was this real sadness. You can sit around and say it's all finished, industry's finished, Glasgow's a ghost town, but the river was still going through, and there is a force there that you can't hold back."

In the event, 'Waterfront' had a big, spacey feel not altogether typical of the rest of the album. *Sparkle* blasted off with a trio of tracks which were crammed with action, the pounding percussion and keyboards of 'Up On The Catwalk' and 'The Book Of Brilliant Things' rocketing the listener straight into the straining vocal and stinging guitar of 'Speed Your Love To Me'. By this point, sensitive punters were calling for oxygen.

The pressure eased a little with the concluding instrumental, 'Shake Off The Ghosts', and the pensive 'Cry Like A Baby', but 'White Hot Day' was also built on the grandest scale, while 'The Kick Inside Of Me' seemed to have been designed as a one-track punk revival. They'd taken a stab at Lou Reed's 'Street Hassle' too, one of its author's most complex and profoundly personal pieces and hardly obvious cover-version material. It didn't work, though Reed himself later claimed to like the version, while listeners unfamiliar with the original seemed not to mind the sludgy, stodgy quality of the Minds' reading. The track sat threateningly at the start of the second side, daring you to sit through it en route to the remaining songs.

It was the *NME*'s Don Watson who first christened Simple Minds "U3" in his review of *Sparkle*, a jibe which went unappreciated by the band. Certainly, anybody who'd first tuned in to Simple Minds with *New Gold Dream* and had then bought its successor must have wondered if they'd stumbled upon a different band with the same name. The album boasted several powerful and original tracks, but there was something frantic and overbearing about its sound. There was too much going on, and the cumulative effect was too intense. If you compared 'Shake Off The Ghosts' with the group's previous instrumental, 'Somebody Up There Likes You', the loss of clarity and precision was marked. After a few listens to *Sparkle*, you felt as though you'd been struck by a low-flying brick.

None of these considerations prevented the disc from vaulting

144

straight to the top of the UK album charts. Also, an excellent remix of 'Speed Your Love To Me' was released as a single in January, just ahead of the album, and it was backed with 'Bass Line', a brilliant instrumental version of 'White Hot Day'. But the Minds still couldn't get a 45 into that elusive Top 10, since 'Speed Your Love' only reached number 20. In March, 'Up On The Catwalk' was selected as the album's third single, but evidently everyone had decided by now that enough was enough and it barely scraped into the Top 30.

In retrospect, *Sparkle In The Rain* stands as a transitional album, a step away from the mesmerizing, instrumentally-based travelling music they'd become identified with towards an outsize form of rock. Their new music was harder, heavier and less subtle. They knew they were moving on towards a new phase, but they hadn't quite got it right yet, which was why *Sparkle* seemed rooted in the past while straining to see into a future which still wasn't entirely clear. The group's still-forming vision was mirrored in an album which was sometimes awkward and ungainly, embracing a fierce rock power but sacrificing the band's familiar grace and sense of space in the process.

Changes were taking place within the fabric of the group. At the beginning of '84, just before the album appeared, they'd flown to Australia and New Zealand to participate in a string of festivals alongside some illustrious acts – Talking Heads, Eurythmics and the Pretenders. It was here that Jim Kerr first met Chrissie Hynde, and rumours of a whirlwind romance between the pair would soon prove well-founded. Hynde would say later that it was love at first sight.

Was it somehow symbolic that at this point Jim Kerr should become involved with an artist who embodied the rock ideals of an earlier generation, a woman plugged directly into the pre-punk mainstream of Dylan and the Rolling Stones? As Kerr saw it, Simple Minds were approaching a crossroads, and the thought doubtless crossed his mind that if America was calling, perhaps the group should go out to meet it.

The spring of 1984 found Simple Minds out on the road across Britain to back up the album release. Virgin's promotional machine had engaged an additional gear on the group's behalf,

145

and the latest photo sessions found the Minds heavily made-up and improbably fashionably dressed. This didn't altogether suit them. Steve Lillywhite took one look at the photos of Mel apparently disguised as Michael Jackson and tactlessly fell off his chair with laughter.

The album's spectacular chart placing and the rush for concert tickets immediately generated interest in the national press, who'd previously ignored Simple Minds because they never appeared on *Top Of The Pops*, didn't get arrested and weren't spotted in nightclubs with highly-paid models. Reporters from the tabloid papers were clamouring to go out on tour with the band, while Kerr was voted "Scotland's Number One Sex Symbol" in a Scottish paper. It was all very odd. Simple Minds wanted the recognition their status deserved, but the kind of coverage they'd begun to get didn't sit easily on them.

Kerr was flattened by a particularly virulent strain of flu halfway through the British tour, and the remaining dates had to be rescheduled. But just before the Minds went back to complete the UK shows, Kerr jetted out to New York and married Chrissie Hynde in a small and unpublicized ceremony in Central Park, attended only by a handful of the pair's closest friends.

He hadn't forewarned the band, apart from Burchill. "I never asked them," he said simply. "Charlie knew. He'd met Chrissie and thought it was a brilliant idea, so that was sufficient. I think people around us could see the shape we were in, and they knew it was going to happen before we actually said so."

Kerr's marriage to Hynde left anybody who knew anything about either of them feeling flabbergasted. Chrissie was well known to be a tough, shrewd character, certainly not somebody given to frivolous love affairs or media games-playing. She was still living with Ray Davies of the Kinks in London, and the pair's daughter, Natalie Rae, had been born the year before. She'd been a fanatical admirer of Davies and the Kinks ever since her teens, and having set her heart on him from a distance, she pursued Davies obsessively until he left his wife to live with her. The story was a slightly chilling indicator of Hynde's formidable willpower. Still, their relationship was known to be a stormy one, with Davies apparently being a more possessive lover than she'd have liked.

Chrissie was steeped in rock 'n' roll music, and had written about it before she started playing it for a living. She'd been born in Akron, Ohio, and had been a journalist for the *New Musical Express* in London during the period when the paper could boast widely-admired writers like Nick Kent and Charles Shaar Murray. At the time, the rock-writer-as-celebrity myth still held some water, with the likes of Kent or the American critic Lester Bangs creating legends around themselves which often out-shone the artists they wrote about.

When punk came along later, it swept away many of rock's long-cherished verities, torpedoing the pompous self-righteousness some writers and many artists had fallen into. At the same time, for better or worse, it demolished much of the resonance and sense of history that had given rock whatever cultural weight it possessed. "Serious" rock criticism would continue, but it would never again have quite the sense of danger or mission it had achieved in its heyday. Its moment had come and gone, and though billions of words would still be spouted extolling the mythic magnificence of Bruce Springsteen, there would always be a sense that the Boss was a happy accident in a downward spiral rather than an indicator of rock music's future.

Perhaps Chrissie Hynde sensed that the graffiti was on the wall for the noble dinosaurs of print. In any event, she wanted success for herself rather than merely to write about other people's stardom, and abandoned her typewriter in 1974 to spend time in rock and R&B bands in both France and her native America. She put her money where her mouth was, and if the glib observation that "music writers are all frustrated musicians" was born out by Nick Kent's band the Subterraneans or Charlie Murray's Blast Furnace and the Heatwaves, neither amounting to much, Hynde's success as a musician would turn the saying inside out. This writer had been a rock star in disguise.

Returning to England, she sang back-up vocals on a Stiff Records' UK package tour, then went on to assemble her own

147

band, the Pretenders. It would have been difficult to find anybody whose musical background was less similar to that of Simple Minds. As the chaotic excess of punk waned, the Pretenders, with their traditional guitar-based melodic rock, began to score hits with singles like 'Stop Your Sobbing', 'Brass In Pocket' and 'Talk Of The Town'. With her distinctively seductive vocals, off-handedly cool stage presence and trade-mark Fender Telecaster guitar, Chrissie seemed to be a female reincarnation of the great rock icons like Keith Richards or Jim Morrison. She had the temperament to match, occasionally acting the prima donna to the hilt, laying into the press when the mood took her while reacting hypersensitively to bad reviews. On the other hand, she would also publicly promote home taping, the technological scourge which has provoked such long and loud whining from the record business in recent years. Chrissie didn't seem to mind making herself unpopular if she had something she wanted to say.

Just as Simple Minds were beginning to explore the possibili-ties of European dance and electronics, the Pretenders were busily re-establishing the mainstream rock tradition which ran from classic bands like the Beatles, the Rolling Stones – or indeed the Kinks – through Dylan, the Velvet Underground or Iggy and the Stooges. The Pretenders' records wouldn't have featured on any of Simple Minds' lists of favourites at that time.

Chrissie was the best part of a decade older than Jim Kerr, and represented an entirely different era of rock music. She'd also proved herself to be hard and resilient, and perhaps it was this side of her character that struck a sympathetic echo in Kerr. A tough and, when necessary, ruthless character himself, Kerr no doubt saw in Hynde's career the kind of determination and sacrifice that would be necessary if his own band were ever to follow the likes of the Pretenders to major stardom.

More than most performers, Chrissie had been through the mill by the time she married Jim Kerr. She'd survived the deaths of fellow-Pretenders James Honeyman-Scott in 1982, and her ex-lover Pete Farndon the following year. Both had succumbed to the classic and needless rock star fate of drink and drugs overdoses. On both occasions, she'd resolutely picked up the pieces, rebuilt the band, and battled on to further chart success. Finally, she was the only remaining member of the original Pretenders, but dismissed the idea of relaunching herself as a solo artist. "I don't think I'm interesting enough on my own to substantiate going solo," she explained simply, if not altogether convincingly.

Up until his wedding to Chrissie, Kerr had never shown the slightest inclination to settle down, and in any case Simple Minds' touring and recording schedule ruled out the idea of home and family in the conventional sense. But perhaps the Minds instinctively regarded their ceaseless travelling as a phase they had to work through before reaching higher, more solid ground. They travelled to get away from their prosaic and unexciting backgrounds, but family and friends would always exert a strong emotional pull on them. Perhaps, in some Catholic sense, they flogged themselves pitilessly in order to earn the rewards they knew they'd eventually achieve.

Once it became clear that the wedding was not, after all, some sort of elaborate hoax, it was obvious that it had been a decisive step for Kerr. He'd taken on a major commitment outside the group, and Simple Minds could no longer be just a bunch of lads together clattering round the world. In a sense, Kerr had always maintained a psychological distance between himself and the others, a necessary precaution for a man upon whom the major decisions about their work and career inevitably devolved.

Brian McGee had perceived this years earlier. "Jim is the main man," he said, one damp Glasgow morning. "At times I used to hate Jim, he's too strong for my liking. No matter how hard everybody works, Jim works the hardest, no matter what anybody says. He thinks all the time about the band, about what's happened and what is to happen. That's why he deserves everything he gets, really, because he's worked harder and he's never stopped really since the word go.

"Sometimes I used to say to Jim, 'I don't want any of the hassles that you have.' As long as I just did my job and enjoyed being with the band, that was good enough for me. We were all chipping in on the basics of organization, but in the end it was

149

Jim who was making the final decisions when the ideas were coming up."

Kerr's marriage gave a concrete form to this apartment. And however Jim and Chrissie looked at it, their wedding also represented a step up for the Minds towards rock's established hierarchy of stardom. It's the way of the world that stars consort with other stars. Still, with both the Minds and the Pretenders on the road, it would be months before Chrissie and Jim had the chance to spend any length of time together, although Simple Minds supported the Pretenders on their American tour later in that summer of 1984.

When Simple Minds finally reached Hammersmith Odeon, where they were booked in for eight sold-out nights, a certain loss of control and distorted perception of reality were in evidence. The curtain went up to reveal Kerr perched unsteadily up a pole, urging the audience to go "up" and "higher" with an offensive born-again zeal. With a few exceptions, such as 'King Is White' or 'The American', the music was loud and leaden, cudgelling the audience into submission. Hitherto, Kerr's performances had been restrained, mysterious and quietly sensual, but suddenly he was cueing in guitar breaks with screams of "*Charlie Burchill!*" and introducing Mel Gaynor as "the finest young drummer in the world". Nobody familiar with the band needed to be lectured on how good they were, while the music had always spoken for itself with great eloquence in the past.

"There was an emptiness around that *Sparkle* promotional thing," Kerr will admit now. Mentions of those Hammersmith shows and the notorious pole go down rather badly with him. "We were very tired on those shows. We weren't good at all. We were disgusted at the psychological shape of things. Two weeks earlier we were brilliant, so that's it. It happens and then it doesn't happen. There was just an emptiness, and do you know what I think it was now? Some kind of . . . a mixture of growing pains and also some kind of void. What I think it was as well was that we had worked non-stop without a rest. We were completely and utterly burned out.

"I was ill then. We had to cancel the shows, if you remember. I was ill in every sense of the word. There was just a kind of

150

emptiness, and it was time to ask questions. I think we had taken a form to the extreme. *New Gold Dream* was very complete, and we didn't want to do more of that. It just seemed totally complete from the first track to the last. It was a growing thing as well. The band and the music were the utmost, but it was time to get involved with people as well – wives, girlfriends and that.

"You're not some kind of a fucking machine. We're from a very traditional background. Family and friendship are big ties. No matter how much we abused them before or took the piss or tried to escape from them, they are the solid roots and the values that we still respect. The thing is, we want to have our cake and eat it. We want to be thoroughly traditional and have all the traditional values, and also be totally contemporary and cosmopolitan. And the clash is there."

CHAPTER 18

The group ended 1984 with a traditional homecoming to Glasgow and a batch of dates at Barrowland, but despite the hysteria in the house, there was a sense that they'd come up against a brick wall. They were undoubtedly successful, and with *Sparkle In The Rain* eventually selling about a million and a half copies worldwide they were more than earning a living. But while they were often portrayed in the British press as the epitome of a new generation of pomp-rockers, they had yet to achieve the kind of sales and, particularly, the American acceptance that would justify the description.

An American tour supporting the Pretenders during the summer hadn't punched home Simple Minds' presence with the potency they might have expected. The fans had plainly come to hear the headliners, while the Minds were largely ignored by the American press. It can't have been easy for Kerr, watching the crowd's ecstatic reception for his wife's band at Madison Square Gardens and wondering what Simple Minds had to do to match it. For the time being, they were neither quite one thing nor the other – they could no longer lay claim to the hipness and mystique they'd enjoyed in their earlier years and which had been a kind of compensation for disappointing record sales, but at the same time they couldn't pretend to be a genuine force in rock's moneyed first division. Paradoxically, they'd spent years working their way up to a genuinely strong level of acclaim in many countries, yet in a sense they were still pariahs. Jumping to the top of the charts in Britain or Australia still meant relatively little in the world's largest market, America.

They'd spent some time writing and rehearsing new material towards the end of the year. They'd booked into Barwell Court in Surrey, a rehearsal studio owned by session bassist John Giblin. While they were there, they were visited by songwriter and producer Keith Forsey, bearing a tape of a song called 'Don't You (Forget About Me)' which he'd written for the soundtrack of a forthcoming film by John Hughes called *The Breakfast Club*.

Simple Minds had already been approached by their record company about recording the song, but what little they'd heard about *The Breakfast Club* had deterred them from wanting to be involved. They suspected it might be crass and juvenile, and entirely out of keeping with the band's image of themselves. A&M Records in America, who distributed Simple Minds' releases in the States, were nonetheless especially keen for them to do it, foreseeing a lucrative and profile-raising connection with Hollywood as well as the inevitable TV and video spin-offs which accompany a hit song from a successful movie. The MTV network had opened up completely new possibilities for artists who were able to grasp the importance of a visual accompaniment to their music.

"We'd made these albums that you would say were great, I would say were great, and for whatever reason in America nobody was getting a chance to hear them," Kerr explained. "They weren't getting on the radio, they weren't getting promoted, they weren't getting taken seriously. It was like we were this weird band from Britain who wouldn't do anything, that would just be a catalogue item at A&M, and you well know we're worthy of a lot more than that."

Simple Minds had long cherished the notion of writing music for film soundtracks. It seemed a bitter irony that when an opportunity presented itself at last, it should be for a project in which they had no interest.

"The whole 'Don't You' thing is an absolute wild twist of fate," said Kerr. "The song presented itself at a time when we had just done this mammoth tour and had had a rest and were kind of hungry to do something. We'd developed this thing of definitely wanting to try and do something in the film world, but the offers weren't exactly pouring in through the door. Which is sad,

153

because I still do think Simple Minds will have our day there – I think our music would be great to movies.

"So this thing presents itself, and initially we hadn't even heard the song, but when we heard it was for a teenage American movie we just said, nah, no way, there's no chance, because there's one of these films coming out every week and they usually just exploit all the usual clichés. There was big record company pressure: 'Try this thing and you'll get offers for more film work.' At the time, there were much bigger names than us pencilled in for the film, we were just going to be one of a series of artists. David Bowie was gonna do a track, so-and-so was gonna do one. We knocked it back, I think, a handful of times."

Then Forsey turned up on the group's doorstep. He'd long been a fan of theirs, and talked them into at least giving 'Don't You' a try. Reluctantly the group agreed, on the condition that Kerr could add some words of his own with the intention of making it sound more like one of their own songs.

"So I went away and I came up with this whole other thing, and it just seemed to be tacked on. It just didn't sit right. At the time we didn't even know if the movie was coming out in Britain or whatever, so we thought, let's try this track and see what it sounds like. We took it away, wrote the intro, wrote the coda with the whole breakdown thing and the la-la-las which are very Simple Minds, and had done the song almost effortlessly. That's the irony – you work your balls off and all this stuff, and we had done this thing in about two hours in a studio outside Wembley. Horrible place, we were desperate to get away from it. We'd done it in about two or three hours – maybe it's a very Catholic thing that for something to be a success you've got to put all your efforts into it and stuff."

The entire process had been so quick and painless that the group more or less forgot all about 'Don't You'. The recording had left so small an impression on them that it seemed improbable that anything lasting would result from it.

Kerr: "We thought it would be part of a movie with about fourteen other big bands. There was no talk at the time we did it of it being a single, and certainly not of it being the title track

154

of the movie. So we did it, went away, started to write the stuff for *Once Upon A Time . . .* and there was this whole kind of a Frankenstein thing, where every record company loved 'Don't You' and radio loved it. It was taking off in America and we were saying, 'Well, it doesn't really matter there because people don't know us.' In Britain and Europe we still wouldn't let them put it out. We'd think, no, it's gonna confuse everyone, people will think this is our next album.''

Yet, as the record became increasingly successful and it looked as though 1985 would be the year in which Simple Minds at last broke through in America, Kerr found it impossible to remain detached and indifferent to it.

''People can say what they like, but as soon as it started to sell, as soon as people started to get immense enjoyment from it, I didn't want to say, 'This is a piece of crap and we could do it with our eyes shut.' Really, we were looking a gift horse in the mouth there. And if you're gonna use it, at least we pulled it off in style. At least it went to number 1 in America, it never went to number 52, and it got a lot of people into *New Gold Dream* and *Sparkle In The Rain.*

''You're brought up with this whole thing of 'I'm an artist and you can't compromise and you shouldn't compromise' – I compromise every single day. That's part of the way the band's changed, as well. I compromise every time I go to the shops, every time I cross the road I compromise. I don't want to wait for the fucking traffic lights to change, I just want to walk, but to get to the other side of the road is a compromise.''

The whole 'Don't You' process evidently caused Kerr considerable angst and soul-searching, though it's difficult to see why in retrospect. 'Don't You' had originally been turned down by Bryan Ferry, who was then hard at work on his *Boys And Girls* album in studios dotted around the earth, and Simple Minds' performance of it was spare and restrained enough to bring the fastidious Ferry to mind. The song subsequently became an overlong singalong affair onstage, but the record was an atmospheric slice of chart pop with a hook which stuck fast after a couple of plays. Simple Minds could hardly have asked for a more suitable vehicle to propel them, finally, onto American

155

radio and into the singles charts. Perhaps what irked Kerr was the fact that after all the band's years of painstaking effort, they'd finally struck it rich with a song written by someone else, although 'Don't You' might easily have been one of their own as far as the casual listener was concerned.

It was the classic mid-eighties multi-media success story. All sorts of people had benefited from both MTV and, latterly, from spin-off soundtracks from movies or TV. Glenn Frey, once in the Eagles, did it with both 'The Heat Is On' from *Beverly Hills Cop* and then with 'Smuggler's Blues', a song spawned by the singer's appearance on hip TV show *Miami Vice*, with its designer clothes and "MTV cops". Prince's *Purple Rain* movie and soundtrack album had turned him from a star into a phenomenon. Duran Duran caused their international stock to soar by persuading somebody to let them write a theme song for the James Bond flick *A View To A Kill*.

Almost everyone who made the kind of records that shot into the American Top 10 and stayed there for months on end had started appearing on movie soundtracks – Phil Collins, Madonna, Mark Knopfler of Dire Straits, Tina Turner, Lionel Richie. All these artists have fingers in a variety of pies and run their careers like prudently-managed investment trusts. They're not just musicians any longer, they're in Entertainment. If Simple Minds were on their way to joining this sort of company, nobody was going to have to worry about where the next house or yacht was coming from.

The success of the single coincided with the group suffering another casualty within its ranks. Derek Forbes, who'd entertained visions of global superstardom ever since the band's earliest days, was fired just as the Minds reached the brink of massive success. Whatever the reasons, this seemed a fairly drastic step. Forbes had been unusual among bass players in that he'd developed a distinct and recognizable sound of his own. His relentlessly-rolling lines for pieces like 'I Travel', 'Love Song', 'Big Sleep' or 'Waterfront' had been as close as Simple Minds came to a lead instrument, and his contributions had often formed the core of the group's songs.

"When Brian McGee left it didn't really pose as much of a

156

problem as when Derek left," said Charlie Burchill afterwards. "He came up with great lines and he had a lot of fans."

Several years earlier, Charlie had offered this assessment of Derek's abilities. "Derek would like to be the technical player and he can play well, but Derek's best points always happen when he's breaking free of being the technician, when he's playing indulgently, if you like, with melody. Then the best side of him comes out. Quite a lot of it can be him thumbing his bass instead of using his fingers because great players play with their thumbs, and all those kind of reasons, but when he's on his own and he knows nobody's listening to him, that's the best time to catch him because you hear him coming out with good things. We've always said about Derek that no matter what, he's always consistent in one thing: he will come up with brilliant things in the end, regardless of all the fucking torment that he went through. At the end of it, it will be there."

Kerr describes the sacking of Forbes as part of the process of the band's growth – painful, but necessary and inevitable. Such emotional pangs as he may have suffered were sublimated for the greater good of the band and its music. You could call it ruthless, or shrewd and farsighted.

"The Forbes thing came at a point where we realized we had come so far, and to better ourselves we would have to go out on limbs and try things. To give ourselves extra drive, we had to go looking for all these other kinds of challenges. I still think in a sense we're looking for these challenges, but Forbes really had given up. He wasn't in a state of mind to come to rehearsals and think about songwriting. He was just basically cruising and it wasn't good enough. He even said it himself . . . the important thing really is kind of the creating and the music. The result isn't the most important thing, it's the drive to create. The result depends on so many things."

Forbes has never been entirely clear about the reasons for his abrupt dismissal, though he's convinced they were by no means all musical. There had been a few incidents over the years where the others had taken him to task for not trying hard enough, but he suspects there were several factors at work. He'd received some bad publicity in the British tabloid press following a

157

drunken fight with his girlfriend, an actress and model called Lindsay, and wonders if Kerr and the others were worried about the band's image as they grew increasingly popular.

It is possible that the group's not insubstantial public profile had already gone to Forbes' head. He'd recently parted company with his fiancée, Kay Melrose, who he'd been with for years, and he clearly enjoyed the band's new and more bombastic style of stage presentation. More recently, Forbes had clashed with Kerr over the video for 'Don't You', which concentrated heavily on Jim and featured the others only fleetingly. Forbes had argued strongly that they were supposed to be a group, not a singer with a few supporting musicians.

The nub of it was that Kerr was the leader of the band, however democratically the music might be written and recorded or however much the group members might claim that band decisions were taken communally. When push came to shove, even Bruce Findlay would have to submit to Kerr's unbending will. Kerr himself has always been aware that the long and demanding task of taking a group to the top of the heap bears little resemblance to a popularity contest, although he wouldn't have said so in so many words.

If Forbes was slacking professionally, it wouldn't do as far as Jim was concerned. A personality clash would have sealed his fate. MacNeil and Burchill, the two other senior members, might have been able to save Forbes from the chop by risking a showdown with Jim, but despite pangs of guilt about their old friend, they acquiesced in the decision to fire him. "Once Jim gets his teeth into something, it comes away in chunks," as Brian McGee once put it. Kerr commands respect, but not always affection.

As it happened, a replacement for Forbes was conveniently at hand in the shape of John Giblin. Gallingly he'd been one of Forbes' musical idols as well as a friend. "We were sitting in this rehearsal place which is owned by John Giblin," said Kerr, "a session player who cannot get in a band for whatever reason for years, who's playing in the hall down the road, and as you go into the rehearsal place you can hear him playing by himself and it's absolutely amazing. And then you've got this guy who won't

158

come to rehearsals, or if he does he's not that interested. In a sentimental way it was a big, big blow, but the music is more important."

Giblin did the decent thing, and refused to accept the Simple Minds job until he'd discussed it with Forbes. The latter took the line that if somebody was going to replace him, he'd prefer it to be Giblin than anyone else. Forbes would later re-emerge as bassist with the singular German group Propaganda, miraculously reunited with Brian McGee on drums. McGee had spent several frustrating years with the Glasgow group Endgames, and was itching for a new challenge.

Giblin's illustrious past as a session musician had included stints with Peter Gabriel and Kate Bush, and he'd played on Phil Collins' solo work as well as with the drummer's band Brand X. He'd also covered a variety of mainstream pop, having toured with the reunited Everly Brothers and recorded with Elkie Brooks and the evergreen Mr Clean of British pop, Cliff Richard. Meanwhile, Simple Minds found that he was a player of high technical accomplishment, given to machine-gun licks and rapid jazz-inflected fingering which deceived the ear and eye. Most of this would have to go if he were to slot into the Simple Minds format. "Sometimes Big John gets embarrassed by what he plays for us because it's so simple," said Mick MacNeil, "but there's no point in getting too complicated, is there?"

Luck suddenly seemed to be running Simple Minds' way, since the first live performance by the revised line-up was at the Philadelphia end of Live Aid in July 1985. This was the first glimpse of Simple Minds that their British fans, especially, had had in a long while, and many of them must have been taken aback by Jim Kerr's hippyish clothes and long hair, while he also seemed to have gained a lot of weight – Chrissie's home cooking, perhaps. There was also the disorienting sight of an entirely unfamiliar figure playing the bass. It was difficult to tell exactly how well (or not) they played, given the questionable nature of the transatlantic satellite hook-up, but 'Don't You (Forget About Me)' was stretched to encourage crowd participation, while a new song called 'Ghost Dancing' sounded like little more than a rough and ready rock 'n' roll jam. The impression was of an American band playing American music.

But Live Aid had a huge knock-on effect for Simple Minds, as it did for the majority of the participants. As the venerated American critic Greil Marcus put it, Live Aid allowed you to see at a glance who counted in rock and who didn't, which suggests he must have missed Adam Ant. Now, Simple Minds had not only their American number 1, they had also established their credentials with the top brass of the international music industry.

In a sense, the Live Aid experience gave them a platform for the next phase of their development. Now, when they sang about love, peace or freedom, the world would listen. The next time Simple Minds went on tour, they would be carrying the Amnesty International banner across continents with them. Live Aid brought about a fundamental shift in the public's attitude to rock and rock stars, and Simple Minds emerged in the afterglow of the event as one of a new generation of bands who slipped a little global consciousness in among the powerchords and massed handclapping.

CHAPTER 19

By the time they played at Live Aid, Simple Minds had more or less finished *Once Upon A Time*, the album which would cement them in place among rock's top people. Again, they'd changed producers, and this time they'd hitched up with Jimmy Iovine and Bob Clearmountain, the Messrs Rolls and Royce of the American industry.

Between them, Iovine and Clearmountain had contributed to some of the weightiest rock records of recent years. Iovine had worked with John Lennon and Patti Smith, and had a long-standing professional relationship with Tom Petty which had begun in 1979 when he co-produced the latter's *Damn The Torpedoes*, the album that brought Petty back from bankruptcy. He'd also produced U2's live mini-album, *Under A Blood Red Sky*, a point which can't have escaped Simple Minds' notice.

Clearmountain, who could play bass and was also something of a prodigy at mathematics, had first shot to prominence with his engineering work with the deluxe disco unit Chic, whose string of dance hits lit up the late seventies. Their recordings, made at New York's Power Station studios, had set new standards in clarity and crispness, while songs like 'Good Times' and 'Le Freak' became synonymous with uptown sophistication. Subsequently, Clearmountain had been hired to clean away some of the sonic sludge which habitually surrounded Rolling Stones recordings and had done a good remixing job on the elderly rockers' *Tattoo You* album. It was a liaison which led to him mixing Mick Jagger and David Bowie's Live Aid single, 'Dancing In The Street'.

Iovine and Clearmountain had appeared, singly or together, among the credits on Bruce Springsteen's records, including *Darkness On The Edge Of Town* and *Born In The USA* (they'd later work on the marathon *Live 1975–1985* set, too). If the producers you used for your records were any guarantee of success, *Once Upon A Time* couldn't fail.

The material on the album had been stripped of many of Simple Minds' earlier subtleties, though the best tracks had a simple weight and clarity, deriving mostly from Mel Gaynor's huge drum rhythms. The sound and structure of the record was a logical development of the ideas which had begun to emerge on *Sparkle In The Rain*. The Minds were no longer introverted manufacturers of atmosphere, mysterious and enigmatic. They had evolved into grandeur-salesmen whose music could only mean one thing.

"It's a very organic way that Simple Minds work, and still do work," said Kerr. "I admit that *Once Upon A Time* was less organic in terms of us knowing we'd love to make a very upfront, thoroughly modern, good-sounding rock record. One that sounds good on CD, radio, in ice-skating rinks and discos. That sounds good full stop, that is very much in focus. Because for us to do that is a challenge, you see."

As Kerr tells it, Simple Minds had been keen to work with Iovine because he'd collaborated with a number of great songwriters in the past. The group had taken seriously earlier criticism that they wrote pieces rather than songs, and that atmosphere was more important in their music than clear-cut structure.

"I think he just helped me to sort of articulate more," said Kerr. "I'm not saying it's terribly articulate. He put the idea of a song in our heads, that encapsulates something in a period of three or four or five minutes, that begins, ends, has a break, has a coda, has a bridge. We realized that we'd never had a bridge in our songs.

"Lillywhite was great to work with as well, but it was great to get away and work with somebody who wasn't necessarily from this kind of English public schoolboy type of tradition. Iovine's dad was a docker, and he's very much a New Yorker. He lives in LA now, but he's kind of urban and also the great thing for me is he's just not musical at all, which I could relate to, not being able to play a note on anything. But his instinct, I think, is great – knowing what the band is capable of, judging people's performances, knowing when that is better or when this could be better. He'd say, 'There should be more heat from it or more sweat from it,' he was very very good like that. And for me, I'm glad of the fact that we're a lot less precious than we were before.''

In other words, Iovine had a knack for spotting pretension or laziness the moment it tried to get up off the floor. "Iovine had a brilliant kind of instinctive thing with me. He's great at looking you in the eye and saying, 'I don't actually think that's the truth, what you just said.' I'd present him with a sheet of lyrics, and maybe I'd spent whatever amount of time on it, and there'd be two lines in it which I'd think were weak or substandard or didn't fit. Because I couldn't think of anything else and because it was killing me, I'd fool myself into thinking, no, they're as good as the rest, you need this for the rest of them to bounce off, kind of thing.

"Iovine would read them and go, 'Yeah, that's great, that's great. What about these two lines here, what do you think of them?' And I'd say, 'I think they're great, I think they're the best lines in the whole song.' And he'd go, 'I don't think you do, actually.' He sees the whole thing as a sporting kind of thing, too. This might sound mercenary, like it's from a sales point of view, but it's not. It's like, 'Right, we need this and we need that. We've got to beat this and we've got to beat that, and we'll give this mix nine and give this one six.' We're very much lads that way as well, so, as I say, it was much better than having the sort of English public schoolboy approach."

Like his predecessors in the Simple Minds' producer's chair, Jimmy Iovine found himself dazzled by the band's confidence and dedication to thrashing out the best possible results. As it happened, he'd admired their music for some time, and there had even been vague talk of hiring him to work on *Sparkle In The Rain*. The American breakthrough had already been made with 'Don't You' by the time *Once Upon A Time* was ready for action, but Iovine had never seen any reason to doubt that the Minds would hit the top of the heap sooner or later.

"I didn't think there was any problem about them becoming successful in America. You have to be *unsuccessful* in America before you can become successful, y'know? I thought they were building it at the right pace, actually. It took a little long, but they'd only had three albums in America, and they'd just had a number 1 record when I worked with them. I assumed at that point with them that everything had come together. I just felt that it had, and I thought it was a good time to work with them. I was really excited for them. We didn't go in and change anything drastically, that's not what happened."

It was a novel experience for Iovine to work with a group whose music was a product of collective effort and input, as opposed to a band who performed material essentially written by one member. Simple Minds hadn't written "normal" songs in the past precisely because of the way the band operated and the way they approached songwriting. Where most artists begin with an acoustic guitar or piano and write a song with a simple, clear structure, Simple Minds' music had been a group activity from the start, with the various members adopting an important shaping role in the proceedings. Their music had been built up layer by layer, the actual sounds of the instruments and the available studio technology being as important to the result as key changes or chord sequences (the *New Gold Dream* instrumental, 'Somebody Up There Likes You', is a case in point).

They'd had to work inwards from the outside, feeling their way towards what other people would regard as accessible or commercial. In this respect, recording 'Don't You (Forget About Me)' had probably been a salutary experience, since it was already a cut-and-dried song before the Minds had come anywhere near it, and they'd had to approach it as professional musicians fulfilling a professional task. The only cover version they'd recorded before that was Lou Reed's 'Street Hassle', which is as unlike a regular rock song as you can get.

"Our songs had these riffs that went on," Kerr said, "and we loved them and we still do, but the challenge was there. I wanted somebody who had worked with songwriters, who

164

instead of just recording a good idea would say, 'That's a good idea, take it away and try to form it.'"

Iovine outlined the differences between recording with the Minds and working with some of his other clients. "With Tom Petty, for example, you're dealing one-on-one with Tom Petty, [Guitarist] Mike Campbell's got something to say, but it's really Tom Petty and the Heartbreakers – the title pretty much tells you what it is. With Simple Minds, it's a band. You see, Tom Petty sits in his house and writes the songs. Therefore he's got the best angle on the song. With Simple Minds, they write the songs together. So to really understand what the song's about, you've got to go to each person that's written that song and really get his slant on it, you know? And you have to get their point of view out on the record as well, so it's a little different."

The group responded to Iovine's straight talking and blue-collar grit. He was spiritually more like a Scotsman than his predecessors, and would have no hesitation in (for example) telling John Giblin, and perhaps Mel Gaynor too, to stop trying to play like some kind of jazz-rock fusion outfit. Giblin and Gaynor loved nothing better than mutual exercises in session-man expertise, but that wasn't what either Simple Minds or Jimmy Iovine were after. Once, Giblin was happily engrossed in a corner of the studio, doodling with some complex chord changes. Iovine abruptly asked him where the jazz section was in the local record store. "I don't know," said Giblin, baffled. "Nor does anyone else, so stop playing that shit," snapped Iovine.

"Sometimes I thought John was playing a little over the top, but that's OK, you've gotta go there," the producer reasoned. "He's a great bass player, and actually his bass parts are a big part of that album. It's always good to push something beyond where it should be and then pull it back a little, and it ends up in an original place rather than a normal place. I actually learned a lot working with all those guys because they're *great* musicians. Simple Minds is some of the best musicians from one place – they have a great, great band, and very few bands can play like that."

Having selected their producers, the band wanted their

165

money's worth. "I enjoyed working with them so much and they let me in so much," Iovine enthused. "When a production arrangement really works is when the artist lets you in. An artist should never pick a producer unless they trust him. If they don't trust him they shouldn't pick him, they shouldn't work with him. It was always ultimately their decision whatever went on the record, but they really heard all the suggestions you made, and they tried 'em. So that's why they're great to work with – they're not frightened. They're very strong about what they want and what they wanna do, and from that place of confidence they're willing to experiment. They're so experimental, and so adventurous. It was a great album to make, it was one of my best experiences."

Although *Once Upon A Time* represented a flowering of Simple Minds' new king-size rock sound, it was still possible to trace the music's roots back a few years. 'I Wish You Were Here' and 'All The Things She Said' were reworkings of backing tracks they'd demoed up in Lincolnshire at the start of 1983, while 'Come A Long Way' resembled another of those pieces but with the tempo doubled.

The best of the new songs were the most spacious and least hurried – 'Once Upon A Time' itself, 'All The Things She Said', 'Alive And Kicking' and 'Come A Long Way', which closed the album on an expectant note which seemed to suggest that there would be plenty more music where this lot came from. All these songs benefited from the deep, fat recorded sound which made even silence feel like something which could be used as a deadly weapon, while the instrumental sounds were strikingly three-dimensional. There was also a minute or two of vintage supercharged Minds at the end of 'Oh Jungleland' (had Kerr consulted Bruce Springsteen about pinching his title?), where the band kicked up a ferocious noise as the track leaped towards the fade.

In addition, the aforementioned first three songs were much enhanced by the diva-like wailing of Robin Clark, who billowed across the mix like a galleon under full sail. Robin was married to Carlos Alomar, David Bowie's long-serving guitarist, and had sung on Bowie's *Young Americans* album in 1975. The record had long been a favourite of Kerr's, and he brought Ms Clark in to the recording sessions apparently with the intention of recapturing something of the Bowie sound. He didn't, actually, but she sounded fine anyway.

Other tracks, like 'I Wish You Were Here' or 'Sanctify Yourself', seemed run-of-the-mill by comparison, while the garish 'Ghost Dancing' – though doubtless ideal for giant outdoor auditoria – could only have been knocked together in some late-night jam session. But *Once Upon A Time* was astutely tailored for its task of conveying the Simple Minds message to millions. The songs addressed themselves, albeit vaguely, to the kind of big moral questions which – as Live Aid had shown – rock audiences felt ready to confront. Kerr sang of "the peaceful revolution and the perfect wave", argued that "hope could spin the whole world round", and introduced us to "a kid called Hope". Frankly, the lyrics were about as woolly as you could get while still announcing your affiliation to the right kind of liberal ideals.

If the music was devoid of the berserk imagination of some of its predecessors, it had a loud simplicity they had by and large lacked. If the exquisite nuances of earlier years had taken a walk, that's because they weren't required this time around. If you'd told Simple Minds they now sounded like the latest addition to the American summertime arena circuit, they'd have clapped you on the back and bought you a drink.

By now, there was probably nothing they could have done to prevent the new album from becoming a monster seller, apart from releasing an LP of folk music or cover versions of bebop classics. They had geared themselves for great things, delivered the right record for the hour, and now the machinery had taken over. All they had to do was ride it to the top. This sense of inevitability was reinforced when 'Alive And Kicking' became their highest-placed single in the UK charts when it reached number 7.

"We realized we were coming to this stage where we were gonna have number 1 albums and we were gonna play to a lot of people," Kerr recollected. "It's like there's this door, and you're tempted – should we go through it or should we hold back? You feel like either knocking on it or phoning somebody up on the other side, be it Dave Gilmour from Pink Floyd or Bruce Springsteen, and saying, 'What do you think?' I'm sure the Pete Townshends and the Jimmy Pages would say 'don't bother', because of whatever happened to their bands and the traumas as soon as they got big, big, big, and reality went out the window.

"But then you think, why should we have to think that we'll blow it in the same senses as they did, necessarily? I think we've got a very, very firm grip on reality that they didn't have. Remember, they had nobody to learn from. There was Elvis and the Beatles, but the Who or Zeppelin were the first of that kind of stadia-and-hamburgers type of group. They didn't know where they were playing, they came in in a helicopter and landed and it's a suitcase full of cocaine and the groupies. I'm not even knocking them, it was just the circumstances at the time. But I think we have them to see what was good and bad about what they were doing. That door is there. With the energy we've got, and we still have a sense of madness in us, you just go through it and deal with it when you get there. It's far more interesting, I think, and far more stimulating as a character, to take that thing on and get punched on the chin sometimes."

Kerr irritably rejected the suggestion that Simple Minds had consciously manufactured a sound designed to appeal to the lowest common denominator among a broad audience. "No, we never ever said that. We just never said it. I think if we had it wouldn't have worked. I think the beauty of it is that it's a kind of instinctive drive. You get subtle clues along the way, but we have never done that. Y'know, you make it sound so kind of easy – 'Oh well, we have to get bigger crowds so we'll just change.'"

Once Upon A Time was released in September 1985, and for fifteen months, Simple Minds took their new music round the world. Everywhere they went, they broadcast the message about Amnesty International too. "Being a father made me think," said Kerr. By now, Chrissie had given birth to another daughter, whom the couple had christened Jasmin. "You start to think of the child's view, not just my children in my case, you start to think of the children of future generations. I think the

168

Amnesty thing more or less coincided with the lyrics that have always been in us but came more and more to the forefront. The idea of these dreams, no matter how naive they are, of some universal freedom, an ideal of universal peace or whatever. It's all right writing about that and singing about it every night, but putting it into practice is something else.

"We gave the audience the benefit of the doubt – is the audience going to accept that? Thankfully they did. You get a cynical eye on you, and I've got a cynical eye that turns on me like hell, with such a strength now, like it never did before. You do a gig in America and the floor is strewn with these Amnesty pamphlets and paper aeroplanes and all that stuff, and you think, 'What is this? This is a lot of crap, I'm completely out of my depth here and it's a wild notion and I'm just being neurotic to think that it actually works.' But first you get the good news from Amnesty saying there's about a dozen cases that because of your gigs are looking really great, then you get a letter from a prisoner in person saying, 'Without doubt death's around the corner.' You just think, fucking hell."

It's a shame, though, that a band has to become so successful before its contributions can make any impact. "That's true, because before that you're blowing your trumpet and nobody can hear you, because you don't have access to prime time news in America. When you realize a month before that 'the single's gonna be number 2 in America which means I get on the biggest network news for three minutes', you have the choice to sit and bullshit about yourself and flog your album and flog tickets, or you get the chance to – I don't mean this in a pompous way – but to communicate or inform.

"I love rock music, which is something I wouldn't have said before. I love the idea of rock music, and the idea of it for me should be primarily entertainment. But there's this huge chunk, I think, in the best of rock music which should be used to inform or communicate or even, dare I say, educate. And therefore 'Sun City' is the ultimate song just now, because in a pleasurable sense, the beat and the melody and the rhythm – it's so urban. It's like the ultimate fucking protest song, and yet the message and the facts are absolutely encapsulated in three or four

169

minutes. There's no doubt what it's about and yet it pleases you no end as well. It's so inspiring."

It seemed to Kerr, too, that the band had needed to grow and develop before it felt able to tackle such significant topics. "Even if we had had the exposure before, I don't think we'd have had the strength to come to a point where you don't feel out of your depth. With the Amnesty thing we fully understood what it was about, whereas with the other various things there's always degrees where maybe you agree with them, and then other things which are out of your understanding. I think we grew towards Amnesty."

The ideals were admirable, and the sceptical view that rock bands can do little more than preach to the converted (mostly for covert personal gain) was given a jolt when a Tamil prisoner in Sri Lanka was released in 1986 as a result of Simple Minds' efforts. At a gig in San Diego they'd appealed for people to join Amnesty and petition on this particular prisoner's behalf.

But some fans of long standing were appalled by the self-congratulation and flatulence of the band's shows. There were interminable versions of 'Waterfront' or 'Don't You (Forget About Me)', the unchanging nightly ritual of the 'Love Song'/ 'Sun City'/'Dance To The Music' medley – however sound the message might be – plus the spectacle of Kerr flinging handfuls of glitter over himself in 'Sparkle In The Rain'. But, of course, any protestations were drowned by the sound of delirious thousands cheering and shrieking. Perhaps the hardest thing to assimilate was Kerr's transformation from the reticent, almost balletic performer of earlier years into a brash, extravagant cheerleader in the American rock 'n' roll mould.

"Yeah, but who are you to say what's weird?" Kerr demands, when confronted with this. "I grew. You can sit and say, well, you grew down or you grew up or you grew fuckin' sideways, but I grew and I changed. So that's tough luck if you can't grasp that."

At Glasgow's Ibrox Park in June 1986, the band triumphantly celebrated their new status with a homecoming which shut the entire city down for the weekend. The reception from the crowd of 80,000 suggested that the government had decreed there'd

170

be free Caribbean holidays and a lifetime's supply of gold bullion for everyone. It was a bold and potentially explosive gesture to play at Ibrox at all, since it's the home ground of the fiercely-Protestant football team, Glasgow Rangers. Traditionally Rangers wouldn't hire a Catholic bartender, let alone a player – until Graeme Souness became manager in 1986 – but here were the mainly-Catholic Simple Minds hoisting the Irish Tricolour flag over the stadium.

The Minds had decided they'd fly a flag for every nationality represented on the day's bill, so there was the Tricolour for Ireland's In Tua Nua and the Waterboys, the Scottish dragon for Hipsway and the Minds themselves, and the Union Jack for Lloyd Cole (though his band, the Commotions, were Scottish). As the Minds' friends and relatives drank themselves into oblivion in the free bar provided by the group – an uncle of Kerr's had even brought his own vial of holy water to sprinkle on the unhallowed Protestant turf – it seemed that miracles were indeed possible, and for those delirious hours, even sectarian divisions ceased to exist. The local boys had conquered the world and now they were back, kicking up the kind of semi-religious fervour U2 had grown accustomed to when they came home to Dublin. Simple Minds had finally arrived, and that was that.

171

CHAPTER 20

For Simple Minds, 1987 was a year of reassessment and pausing for breath. It was a time to reflect on the group's achievements and the effort which had gone into making them happen. They went back to Scotland (or in Mel Gaynor's and John Giblin's case, London) and reestablished contact with family and friends.

Charlie Burchill and Mick MacNeil had each bought houses in the Glasgow area, though while Mick lived with his long-term girlfriend Hanna, Charlie moved his family into his new home while he continued to look for a place of his own. A couple of newspapers had floated a rumour about Mick and Hanna's imminent marriage, which didn't seem impossible but in fact hadn't been planned. Charlie, meanwhile, was still seeing his Italian girlfriend Gabriela, who he'd first met some four years earlier. Perhaps even the restless guitarist was beginning to consider the possibility of slowing down a little.

Jim Kerr was faced with the responsibilities of marriage and fatherhood, obligations which can be temporarily kept at arm's length during prolonged periods of touring. Although the Minds were off the road, the Pretenders weren't, and Kerr found the absence of both Chrissie and the kids, Jasmin and Natalie, difficult to cope with. Jim admits that he can only face changing nappies as a last resort, and Chrissie took the girls with her on the road, where two nannies helped her look after them while she also got on with the job of running a rock group. Jim would fly out to catch up with the Pretenders when he could, perhaps combining the trip with local interviews, but it was

172

hardly the same as a quiet family evening round the living-room fire.

"Ultimately you're gonna get it on the chin, and I'm getting it on the chin just now," he said, one day in early summer at his flat overlooking the Forth Bridge. It's a curious fact of Jim and Chrissie's marriage that even when they're both in Britain, he prefers to head for his flat in Scotland while she'd rather stay in London's Maida Vale. The northern air seems to suit Kerr, and he spoke lucidly and with a confidence which had always been in him, but which had only recently shown through in his outward manner. He wasn't quite twenty-eight.

"You can't just drift through, it just takes its toll. It might take its toll when you're seven or eight years old and you lose your parents, or something. I've very, very lucky, and I'm not saying that in a smug sense. I've only realized I'm lucky because the more and more I get out and talk to people, I see when they start talking the hardships they have. You just think everybody gets dealt the same card. You don't dare to think you're lucky or extreme or whatever.

"I don't mean to sound like a social worker, but I have a lot of mates in Glasgow now. I'm much more intact in reality, and I think it's got a lot do to with the way I lead my life just now. Before, I was into having reality way around the corner, but I am actually in Glasgow quite a lot. The worst kind of slagging I've ever had in my life happened yesterday, when the *NME* called me an expatriate. That's the pits.

"But I've spent a lot of time in Glasgow in the past two years, actually on any days off I've been there or I've been here, and I've managed to work on friendships and stuff with schoolmates and old pals, building them up again. The problems I have are absolutely miniscule compared to the problems they have. And I don't mean that in a condescending way – it's just the truth."

While Jim Kerr now seems eager to demonstrate that he's just like the next man after all, the whole point of being a rock star has always been to prove that you aren't ordinary or run-of-the-mill. Kerr has worked to preserve his local ties, but he and Chrissie also spent New Year, 1986/7 in New Jersey with Bruce Springsteen. Kerr wouldn't be human if he didn't enjoy the fruits of his labours, but he's insulated from the kind of day-to-day problems his peers and contemporaries must face.

Perhaps this desire to reestablish touch with past roots and contacts could also be discerned in the band's live double album, *Live In The City Of Light*, released in May. A product of the 1985/6 tour, the album presented a handy compendium of Simple Minds' best-known songs, exquisitely recorded and tastefully edited. The tedious, overblown aspects of the live shows were conspicuously absent, and songs which had lasted fourteen minutes had been trimmed to a manageable four or five.

The band had been worried that 'Someone Somewhere (In Summertime)' had lost its original spark, and had managed to refurbish it with an overdubbed violin part by Lisa Germano, who Kerr had originally spotted on a TV show in the States. Her swinging, country-flavoured lines should have sounded ludicrously out of place amidst Simple Minds' high-tech mega-rock, but instead her playing added some reflective warmth to what might otherwise have been a rather plodding performance. Somewhere, there exists a tape of Kerr, Burchill, MacNeil, Lisa Germano and Garth Hudson, veteran organist from The Band, playing a version of 'Song To The Siren', the Tim Buckley tune memorably recorded by This Mortal Coil.

Nothing so intimate as that featured on *Live In The City Of Light*, though 'New Gold Dream' appeared in a new, mysterious arrangement, and there was a powerful performance of 'Alive And Kicking'. Some of the material you could live without, like the inevitable 'Ghost Dancing' which had been disastrously programmed as track one, side one, but there was a compactness and discipline in many of the performances which went some way to challenging the pomp-rock tag.

"It isn't meant to capture that whole thing," said Kerr, referring to the scarf-waving singalongaJim dimension of the band. "Three months later, you can look back at the shows and say, yeah, that was too much or that was overblown and that was wrong, the same as you can say that was right and this was it. It isn't meant to capture the exact thing – I think it's meant to capture the essence and the atmosphere. It comes from the idea of people who are fans of the band, and if they were to close their

174

eyes the album should take them pretty much to the gig. And I have the utmost confidence that it does. So it's without doubt a success.''

While being a desirable (and cheap) souvenir for fans who'd attended the shows, it might also have been assembled with the aim of persuading doubters that an authentic heart still beat at the core of Simple Minds. It suggested that the Minds needn't be all bluster and bombast after all.

More remarkably, Derek Forbes had been recalled to overdub a new bass part on 'Someone Somewhere (In Summertime)', though he isn't credited on the sleeve. He also added new parts to live recordings of 'Glittering Prize' and 'Celebrate', originally cut at Barrowlands in Glasgow when Derek was still in the band. These were included on the B-side of 'Promised You A Miracle' when it was released as the first single from the live album in June 1987.

There had long been pangs of remorse within the band about Forbes' sacking, at least with Burchill and MacNeil, who'd always maintained close contact with the bassist after the split. When they're all back in Scotland, Charlie, Derek and Brian McGee often play football together on Sundays for a team called Craigmarloch, which also happens to be the name of Forbes' new house.

When the Minds had played at Dublin's Croke Park in June 1986, Forbes had joined them onstage for a large chunk of the set. As members of the road crew brushed away tears of emotion and U2 cheered from the wings, Forbes plugged in and played on 'Big Sleep', 'The American', 'Someone Somewhere (In Summertime)' and 'New Gold Dream'. John Giblin slotted in alongside him at first, then sneaked off and left him to it. The permanent re-hiring of Forbes is improbable, though both he and Brian McGee look set for a revitalized future with Propaganda, who have finally emerged from a long and punishing lawsuit with the ZTT label. At the time of writing, they were on the brink of a new recording contract and planning to record an album of new material.

In The City Of Light set off at a blistering pace for the top of charts almost everywhere, going straight in at number 1 in the UK, following copious advance orders. U2's album *The Joshua Tree* had preceded its release by a couple of months, and it

175

seemed that the two bands were in some kind of friendly competition for a similar audience with some of the same ideals and aspirations. Perhaps Simple Minds even benefited from the massive slipstream U2 began to generate as they proceeded across America and around the world, challenging Springsteen as the world's greatest rock act. After fans had bought *The Joshua Tree*, the next best thing was probably a Simple Minds album although *In The City Of Light* ultimately put up a disappointing chart performance in America. Jim Kerr suggested this was because U.S. radio stations are much less inclined to play live recordings than studio ones.

Jimmy Iovine still thought *In The City Of Light* was the smartest move the band could have made. "I think they did a great job. I think it's a really important album for them in America, because it will help people in America understand the history of the band. A lot of Americans just know them from 'Don't You' and from then on. So now they can go back with good recordings of those older songs, and it will establish the history of the band here a little bit."

So were the comparisons between U2 and Simple Minds valid? "The reason why there are comparisons between them is because there is such a lack of great bands today, and there is such a lack of originality," said Iovine. "U2 and Simple Minds put out the spirit of the sixties and you have a completely original band making those records. There are so few original bands that have the whole spirit of what this whole game was originally about, that's why people are comparing them. There's a spirit behind their music and a theme for it. There's a culture within each band, and that is why they get compared. There's a serious depression of that in the industry today."

The adulatory Iovine anticipates more and greater things from both groups, and not just because he hopes to produce Simple Minds again. "They've just begun, they really have, and again that's like U2. It's because they're young and they're wanted, and they want to get better. That's what a lot of bands are missing – they want to be great, but they don't want to get better. A lot of bands just think about sounding like somebody else, and that's not what Simple Minds are about."

Some of Jim Kerr's current thinking reflects something of Iovine's observations about the spirit of Simple Minds. "Becoming a father made me much more political in the true sense of the word," he pondered. "I guess what it is really is that suddenly you've got to think about the world existing when you're gone, and therefore all these things start coming into it."

This is all a long way from the early days at the Mars Bar, and far removed from the Transit-van years when the band rollicked across Europe, relying on luck and Brian McGee's driving. As rock music has grown into a big business and refused to die before it got old, so the people for whom it's been their life have had to adjust, compromise or reevaluate with the passing years. Paul McGuinness, U2's manager, has already addressed the problem. "Nothing would surprise me less than to see them as 50-year-old men, making some kind of album," he said of Bono and the boys. "I mean, what do you do when you're an *ex*-member of a rock 'n' roll band?"

One of the things that keeps Jim Kerr and Chrissie Hynde at least spiritually united, despite the miles that frequently separate them, is a concern for the way the environment is being systematically polluted and degraded. Arguments rage in their household about nuclear waste, rivers and oceans being too toxic to swim in, and the unnecessary killing of animals (Chrissie even has nightmares about the latter). Both their bands were scheduled to play at the giant Greenpeace concert in Moscow, and Kerr believes that the party politics that bedevil British life serve only to blind everybody to the real issues, which are global and ecological rather than local and partisan. "The Green party in Germany I think are brilliant," Kerr notes. "The end of the world is worth being militant about." The couple don't want their kids to grow up in an amoral, poisoned world, and they see their music as one way of trying to prevent that from happening.

All well and good, but you can't help wondering what happened to the rip-it-up good times of primitive rock 'n' roll. Perhaps only the Beastie Boys know. Rock no longer automatically means "youth". It will never again be the delinquent, innovative medium it once was and it hasn't managed to bring down a government yet, but it's unwise to underestimate its potency in articulating broad communal emotion. The danger arises when the idealistic zeal aroused by major rock acts gets turned around or manipulated for political or commercial ends.

It's a problem many artists in the post-Live Aid environment face, and for the millions of fans who adore Springsteen or U2, there will always be dissenting voices pointing to evidence of hype, hypocrisy or profiteering. It's never going to be easy to accept a lofty moral tone from showbiz superstars pocketing hundreds of thousands of dollars per night, even if they do give a small percentage of it away to good causes. And there's an obvious contradiction between expressing apparently radical beliefs while making music that appeals to broad, mainstream tastes.

The snag is, the people behind the music eventually disappear, partly for their own protection and mainly because there isn't enough of them to go round. Bruce Springsteen, ostensibly the great blue-collar populist, now seems as remote and untouchable as some Venetian Doge of the Renaissance, generating monstrous biographies about himself which merely fuel the myth. A *World In Action* documentary about U2, shown on television in Britain in 1987, appeared to demonstrate that the Irish quartet really are seen as the Second Coming in the Emerald Isle, even if the band's members regard the idea with suspicion.

The marketing of an artist through multiple and interlocking mass-media can create a phenomenon of awesome, unmanageable proportions, and the potential for mismanagement or exploitation is going to land somebody in serious trouble someday. The performers themselves may or may not remain unchanged by all the brouhaha (such adulation must go to your head, but access is so tightly controlled that there's no way of knowing for sure). It's certain that the dimensions of success which have become possible are too massive for mere humans to live up to. As for the consumers, all you can do if you don't like your entertainment on that sort of scale or your emotions being pumped up by a dot on a stage half a mile away is find somebody less famous to listen to.

Simple Minds have become big, but aren't yet expected to

walk on water unless they're playing in Glasgow. *Once Upon A Time* sold four million copies, but *Born In The USA* totalled eighteen million. "I speak to young journalists in Europe and they treat me like I'm Pete Townshend, or something," grinned Kerr. "But we only feel that we're at the end of the first phase, and there's so much more to go for in terms of being better songwriters, making better records, doing better shows, being more articulate.

"There's still this idea of rock being the young thing and the teenage thing, and your twenties to your thirties are your good years. In every other single art, nobody even blossoms until they're well into their thirties – I'm talking about authors or painters or what have you. And really, up till now, we've been writing almost by proxy, and now it's time to be concrete, be involved, write from experience."

The next period in Simple Minds' career will probably focus on recording rather than on live work. An album of instrumentals has been under sporadic discussion probably since as long ago as 1980, and looks as though it may finally come to fruition. "We want to make much better records and many more records," said Kerr. "Towards the end of making an album you feel you're getting to know how the whole thing works, then in a sense you've got to down tools. Then you go on tour for fifteen months, then you take six months to write. By the time you get back in the studio it's almost three years later, and you've forgotten what you learned and the studio's alien to you. No wonder Prince makes records like he does – he's never out of the studio, apart from being a genius before he went in."

Finally, Simple Minds are at a stage where they have the luxury of choice, and time to think about it. Kerr points out that it was only in 1985 that the group began to get themselves out of the debts they'd accumulated during the earlier part of their career.

"The truth is, there are two phases of Simple Minds. The first – and I don't know when it ended – is one of a band making music that I would say was of a voyeuristic nature. Like with *Empires And Dance*, being in Paris or Munich and there's bombs going off. You're looking around and you're writing it down, and you're not coming out and saying whether it's good or bad or indifferent. You're just talking about a series of events. And then with the next phase, and I don't know how or why it changed, but undoubtedly it did and it's in my personality as well, is much more physical and open.

"I think we're at a great period because of what we've learned, the good stuff, the bad stuff, whatever. I don't want to be anything else, other than part of a musical group."

This must be music to Bruce Findlay's ears, and Findlay's commitment to Simple Minds clearly paid off in the long run. Now, he not only has a new house and a new Jaguar but has expanded Schoolhouse Management's roster of clients to encompass China Crisis (originally signed up after they supported Simple Minds on their late-1982 British tour), new Scottish band the Silencers, and TV presenter and journalist Muriel Gray. A few years back, he summed up Simple Minds and his experiences of living and working with them in words which may or may not ring just as true now. His remarks undoubtedly hit upon a kernel of truth, and in any event, he'll never express it better.

"We are just on the verge of madness. We're on the verge of becoming ridiculously commercial and we've always been on the verge of becoming ridiculously weird or obscure. I like Simple Minds and I like my lifestyle with them because we live right on the edge. We do live in a wee bit of a twilight zone. On the one hand we appear to be terribly conventional and nice, but some of the things that are said or things that go on on the road are not quite so conventional. A lot of people are hypocritical – they pretend to be one thing when they are the other. We pretend to be neither, and we're both."

DISCOGRAPHY

SINGLES

JOHNNY AND THE SELF ABUSERS

Saints And Sinners/Dead Vandals
Chiswick NS22 November 1977

SIMPLE MINDS

Life In A Day/Special View
Zoom-Arista ZUM 10 March 1979

Chelsea Girl/Garden Of Hate
Zoom-Arista ZUM 11 June 1979

Changeling/Premonition
Zoom-Arista ARIST 325 January 1980

I Travel/New Warm Skin
Zoom-Arista ARIST 372 (also limited edition flexi-disc including Kaleidoscope and Film Theme Dub) October 1980

I Travel/Kaleidoscope/Film Theme
Zoom-Arista 12 inch single ARIST 12372 October 1980

Celebrate/Changeling
Zoom-Arista ARIST 394 February 1981

Celebrate/Changeling/I Travel
Zoom-Arista 12 inch single ARIST 12394 February 1981

The American/League Of Nations
Virgin VS 410 May 1981

The American/League Of Nations
Virgin 12 inch single VS 410-12 May 1981

Love Song/This Earth That You Walk Upon
Virgin VS 434 July 1981

Love Song/This Earth That You Walk Upon
Virgin VS 434-12 July 1981

**Sweat In Bullet/Twentieth Century Promised Land/
Premonition/League Of Nations**
Virgin VS 451 double single October 1981

**Sweat In Bullet/Twentieth Century Promised Land/
League Of Nations/In Trance As Mission**
Virgin 12 inch single VS 451-12 October 1981

I Travel/30 Frames A Second
Arista ARIST 448 January 1982

I Travel/I Travel (Live)/30 Frames A Second
Arista ARIST 12448 January 1982

Promised You A Miracle/Theme For Great Cities
Virgin VS488 April 1982

**Promised You A Miracle/Theme For Great Cities/
Seeing Out The Angel**
Virgin 12 inch single VS 488-12 April 1982

Glittering Prize/Glittering Prize Theme
Virgin VS 511 (7 and 12 inch) August 1982

Someone Somewhere (In Summertime)/
King Is White And In The Crowd
Virgin VS 538 November 1982

Someone Somewhere (In Summertime)/
King Is White And In The Crowd/Soundtrack For Every Heaven
Virgin 12 inch single VS 538-12 November 1982

Waterfront/Hunter And The Hunted
Virgin VS 636 (7 and 12 inch) November 1983

Speed Your Love To Me/Bass Line
Virgin VS 649 (also picture disc VSY 649) January 1984

Speed Your Love To Me (extended version)/
Speed Your Love To Me/Bass Line
Virgin 12 inch single VS 649-12 January 1984

Up On The Catwalk/Brass Band In Africa
Virgin VS 661 (also picture disc VSY 661) March 1984

Up On The Catwalk (extended version)/
Brass Band In African Chimes
Virgin 12 inch single VS 661-12 March 1984

Don't You (Forget About Me)/Brass Band In Africa
Virgin VS 749 (also picture disc VSY 749) April 1985

Don't You (Forget About Me)/Brass Band In African Chimes
Virgin 12 inch single VS 749-12 April 1985

Alive And Kicking/Alive And Kicking (instrumental)
Virgin VS 817 September 1985

Alive And Kicking/Alive And Kicking (instrumental)/
Up On The Catwalk (instrumental)
Virgin 12 inch single VS 817-12 September 1985

Sanctify Yourself/Sanctify Yourself (instrumental)
Virgin SM1 January 1986

Sanctify Yourself (extended version)/Sanctify Yourself (dub)
Virgin 12 inch single SM1-12 January 1986

All The Things She Said/Don't You (Forget About Me)
Virgin VS 868 April 1986

All The Things She Said/Don't You (Forget About Me)/
Promised You A Miracle (US remix)
Virgin 12 inch single VS 868-12 April 1986

Ghostdancing/Oh Jungleland
Virgin VS 907 November 1986

Ghostdancing/Ghostdancing (instrumental)/Oh Jungleland/
Oh Jungleland (instrumental)
Virgin 12 inch single VS 907-12 (also on CD MIKE 907)
November 1986

Promised You A Miracle (Live)/
The Book Of Brilliant Things (live)
Virgin SM2 (also on 10 inch SM 2-10) June 1987

Promised You A Miracle (live)/
The Book Of Brilliant Things (live)/Glittering Prize (live)/
Celebrate (live)
Virgin 12 inch single SM 212-12 (also on-single MSC 212) June 1987

ALBUMS

Life In A Day
Zoom-Arista ZULP 1 April 1979
Tracks: Side 1 – Someone/Life In A Day/Sad Affair/All For
You/Pleasantly Disturbed. Side 2 – No Cure/Chelsea Girl/
Wasteland/Destiny/Murder Story

Real To Real Cacophony
Zoom-Arista SPART 1109 November 1979
Tracks: Side 1 – Real To Real/Naked Eye/Citizen (Dance Of Youth)/Carnival (Shelter In A Suitcase)/Factory/Cacophony/ Veldt. Side 2 – Premonition/Changeling/Film Theme/Calling Your Name/Scar

Empires And Dance
Zoom-Arista SPART 1140 September 1980
Tracks: Side 1 – I Travel/Today I Died Again/Celebrate/This Fear Of Gods. Side 2 – Capital City/Constantinople Line/ Twist-Run-Repulsion/Thirty Frames A Second/Kant-Kino/ Room

Sons And Fascination/Sister Feelings Call
Virgin V2207/Virgin OVED 2 September 1981
Tracks (Sons): Side 1 – In Trance As Mission/Sweat In Bullet/70 Cities As Love Brings The Fall/Boys From Brazil. Side 2 – Love Song/This Earth That You Walk Upon/Sons And Fascination/ Seeing Out The Angel
(Sister Feelings) Side 1 – Theme From Great Cities/The American/ 20th Century Promised Land. Side 2 – Wonderful In Young Life/League Of Nations/Careful In Career/Sound In 70 Cities
[A compilation of tracks from Sons/Sister Feelings, Empires And Dance and Real To Real Cacophony, called THEMES FOR GREAT CITIES, was released by Stiff Records in the USA, cat. no. TEES 2. A Canadian release of SISTER FEELINGS CALL (VEP 311) comprised 70 Cities/Careful In Career/Wonderful In Young Life/Seeing Out The Angel/Sound In 70 Cities, with cassette version (VEP4 311) additionally including This Earth That You Walk Upon]

Celebration
Arista compilation album SPART 1183 February 1982
Tracks: Side 1 – Life In A Day/Chelsea Girl/Premonition/Factory/ Calling Your Name. Side 2 – I Travel/Changeling/Celebrate/ Thirty Frames A Second/Kaleidoscope

New Gold Dream
Virgin V2230 September 1982 (US – A&M SP4928)
Tracks: Side 1 – Someone Somewhere In Summertime/Colours
Fly And Catherine Wheel/Promised You A Miracle/Big Sleep/
Somebody Up There Likes You. Side 2 – New Gold Dream
(81-82-83-84)/Glittering Prize/Hunter And The Hunted/King Is
White And In The Crowd

Life In A Day
Virgin VM6 October 1982
Real To Real Cacophony
Virgin V2246 October 1982   [reissues of original
Empires And Dance   Arista releases]
Virgin V2247 October 1982
Celebration
Virgin V2248 October 1982

Sparkle In The Rain
Virgin V2300 February 1984 (US – A&M SP6 4981)
Tracks: Side 1 – Up On The Catwalk/Book Of Brilliant Things/
Speed Your Love To Me/Waterfront/East At Easter. Side 2 –
Street Hassle/White Hot Day/"C" Moon Cry Like A Baby/The
Kick Inside Of Me/Shake Off The Ghosts

Once Upon A Time
Virgin V2364 (also picture disc VP 2364) January 1986 (US – A&M
SP5092)
Tracks: Side 1 – Once Upon A Time/All The Things She
Said/Ghost Dancing/Alive And Kicking. Side 2 – Oh Jungleland/
I Wish You Were Here/Sanctify Yourself/Come A Long Way

In The City Of Light
Virgin SMDL 1 May 1987 (US – A&M SP6850)
Tracks: Side 1 – Ghost Dancing/Big Sleep/Waterfront/Promised
You A Miracle. Side 2 – Someone Somewhere In Summertime/
Oh Jungleland/Alive And Kicking. Side 3 – Don't You (Forget
About Me)/Once Upon A Time/Book Of Brilliant Things/East At
Easter. Side 4 – Sanctify Yourself/Love Song-Sun City-Dance To
The Music/New Gold Dream